Sheila Steinberg and Kate Dooner

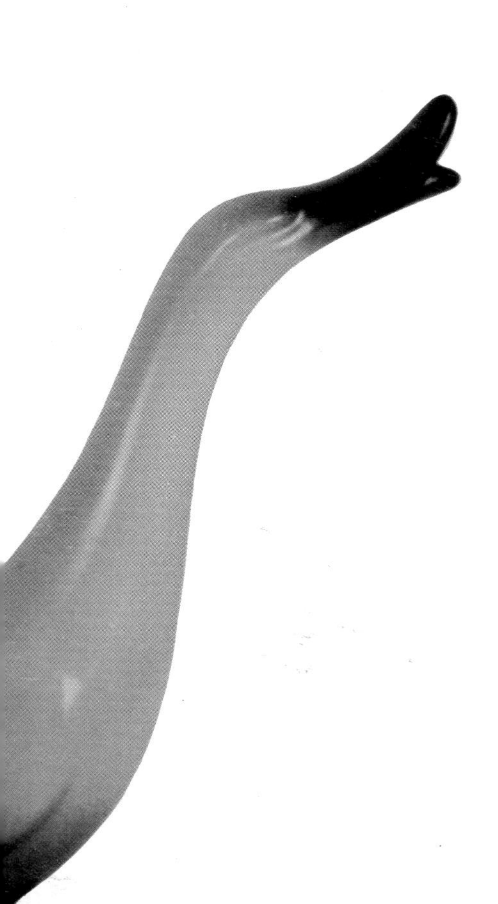

fabulous FIFTIES

Designs for Modern Living

77 Lower Valley Road, Atglen, PA 19310

Acknowledgments

Thanks to the many collectors and dealers who have so generously contributed their knowledge and inspiration. They are too numerous to list without omissions but this book would not have been possible without them. Special thanks to my family and friends for their support throughout this endeavor.

Also thanks to the following people: The Schiffers for tailor making this project for me and making it a reality; Kate Dooner for her excellent work on the text and captions; Douglas Congdon-Martin for his wonderful photographs and John Hylton for his brilliant design work.

Sheila Steinberg
New York
March, 1993

Dedication

To:
Irma & Harold, Ken & Nancy,
Alex & Julie & Norman

Library of Congress Catalog Number: 92-63105.
Book design by John Hylton
Assistant designer, Sheila Steinberg.
Photography by Douglas Congdon-Martin.

Printed in the United States of America
ISBN: 0-88740-468-5

Published by Schiffer Publishing, Ltd.
77 Lower Valley Road
Atglen, Pennsylvania 19310
Please write for a free catalog.
This book may be purchased from the publisher.
Please include $2.95 postage.
Try your bookstore first.

We are interested in hearing from authors with book ideas on related subjects.

CONTENTS

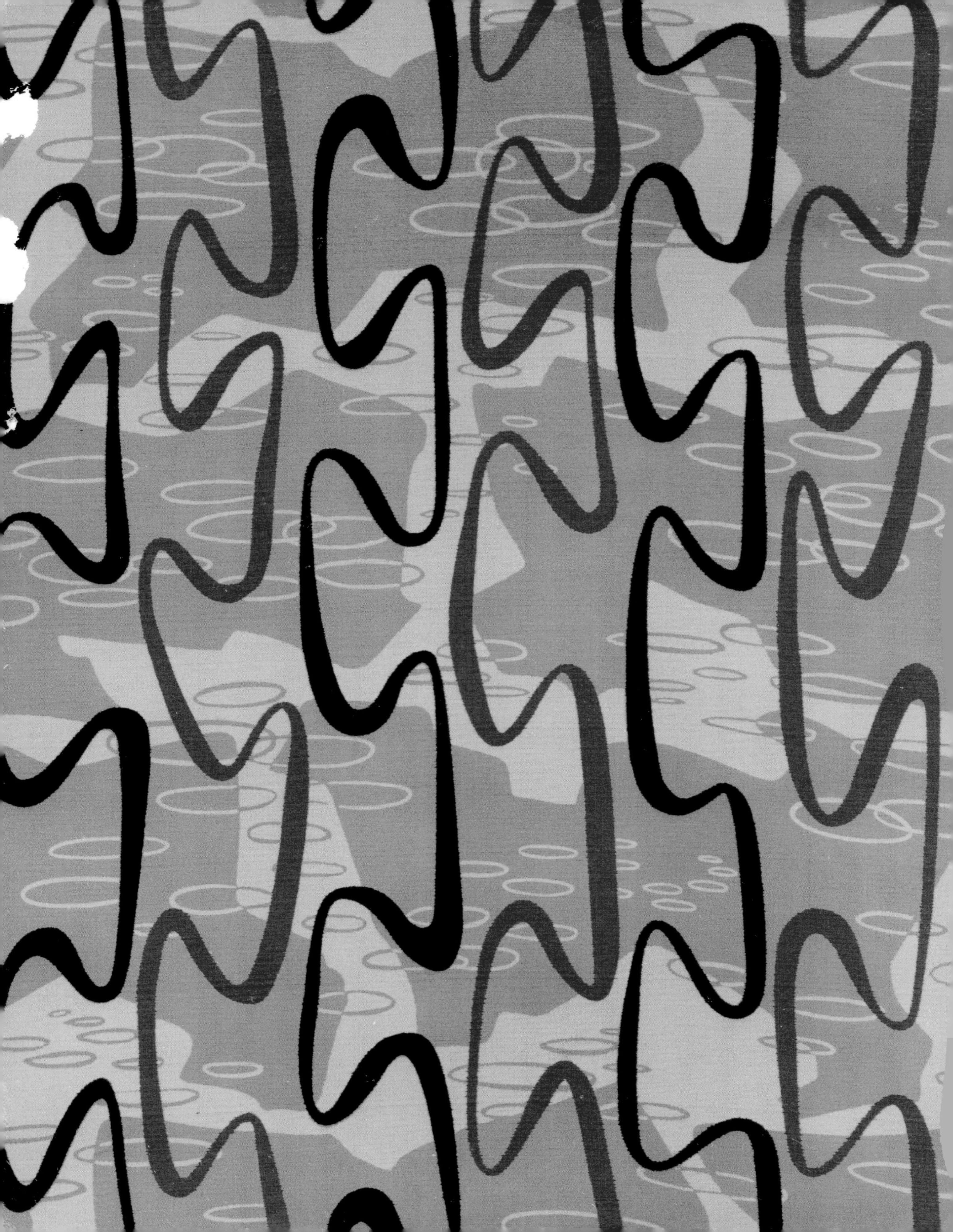

PREFACE

Have you ever felt as though you have two different personalities? When confronted by the unwary, author Sheila Steinberg has been known to introduce herself as her second personality, Adelina Catalina. Adelina is a child of the fifties, born in Vinylhaven, Maine. She ran away from home at a very young age, escaping on a fishing boat, but during a storm was thrown overboard. She was saved several hours later but failed to thank her rescuers, and instead screamed out "where's my plastic purse!?!" The rescue boat sailed on to Catalina Island (hence Adelina Catalina Productions, Sheila's business name) and Adelina headed straight for Melrose Avenue in Los Angeles. The rest is history.

Adelina is a child, fun and creative. Sheila is the adult, left behind to pay the bills.

In all seriousness, about ten years ago, Steinberg met her friend Norman and his encouragement became part of the inspiration for a ten year quest for the very best of those treasures designed in the 1940s and 1950s. The focus for her collection has been the light-hearted, humorous, whimsical and artistically designed items from the period. The design firm of Adelina Catalina Productions has grown to help assemble and place collections for an international clientele. Many of those collections have been exhibited in New York at the Modernism and Triple Pier shows. Steinberg's collection of vintage costume jewelry was discussed by Nancy Hoving in an article which appeared in *Connoisseur* Magazine. All of the items photographed for this book are from the collections of Adelina Catalina Productions. The vast majority date approximately from 1945 through 1960. Precise dating is often difficult.

Steinberg claims that one of her strongest motivations for collecting the designs from this period is that they are both affordable and available. She can afford the very best—even if it is the finest and most artistic vinyl handbag ever manufactured.

Many of the items collected are utilitarian, used by people every day. Sheila requires that each item have a very strong and wonderfully artistic design, and the more whimsical the better. The brilliant designers who worked during this era, most of whom remain unknown today, created a body of work remarkable for its artistry and creativity. It is important to Sheila that she can share this work so it may be further appreciated today. Bon Voyage!

1 A squiggle pattern on fabric, abstract.

2

INTRODUCTION

3

The post World War II period is sometimes referred to as the "baby boomer era," or the "fabulous fifties," with a new generation that had it all. Popular culture for the Western World took a turn in the fifties, beginning in the United States. Since they were furthest from the war, Americans were the least affected by its devastation. People in the United States had the advantage, and popular culture had the opportunity to flourish. New consumer goods were mass produced, and soon this culture spread to the other countries. In fact, the late-'40s and early-'50s were probably the only time that America led Europe where mass culture was concerned. By the 1960s, a reassertion of European influence came about, in terms of cultural dominance. The 1950s brought the United States leadership in terms of cultural goods!

2 Hatboxes with "Doreé," "Jeanne Tête," and an abstract design.

3 Round poodle plate by Sascha Brastoff. 11.5" diameter.

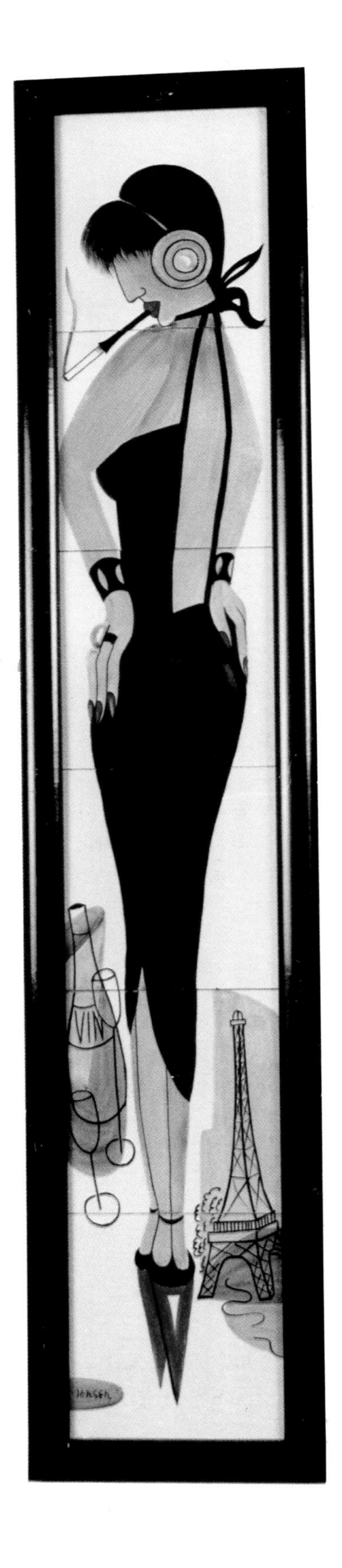

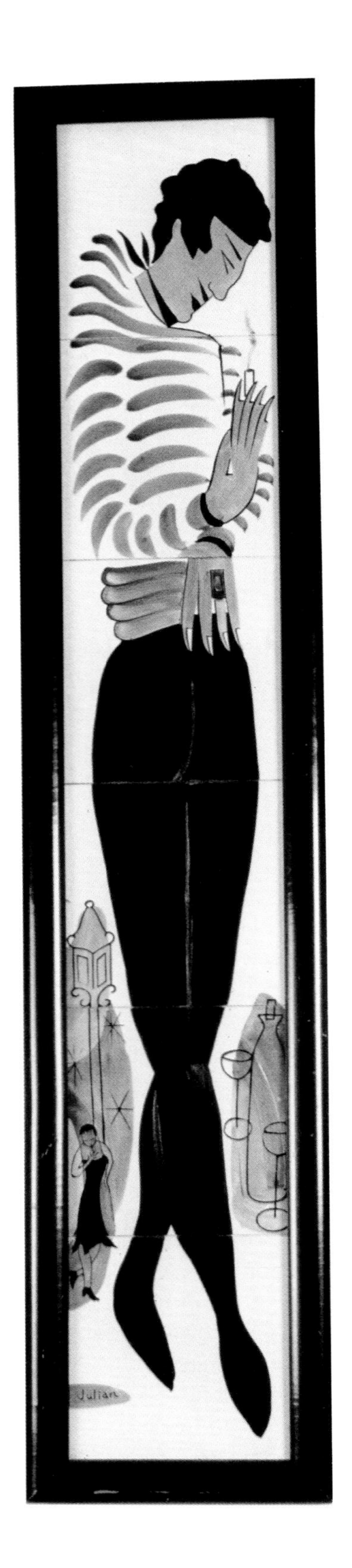

4

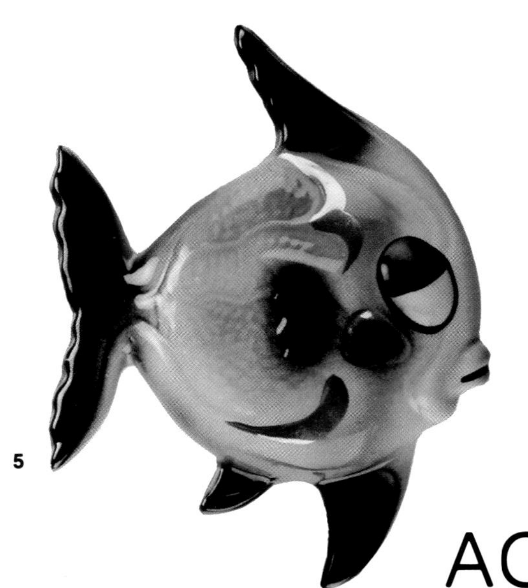

5

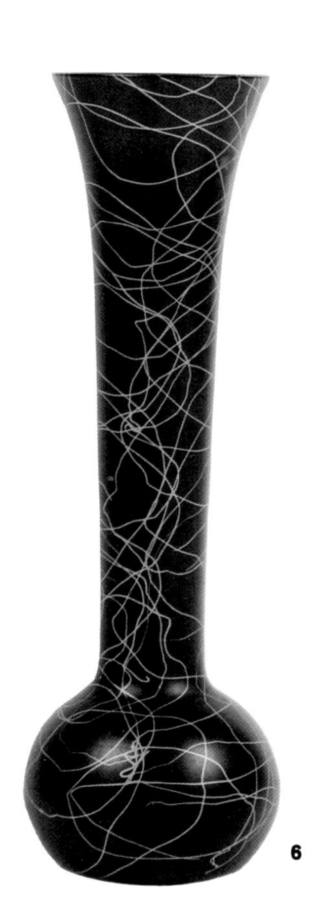

6

ACCESSORIES FOR THE HOME

7

The American home itself took a complete turn in decoration as households became equipped with major appliances never known before. What had been a futuristic world in the 1930s was now being realized as housewives could do their work at the push of a few buttons. Dishwashers, clothes washers and dryers, electric blenders, and televisions were more readily available, and a growing majority were able to buy them. The prosperity in the post-war era enabled many to have these conveniences for the first time.

Widespread buying, however, caused a great change in family life. A new middle class emerged in the suburbs. People could afford the luxury of living outside the city and bought a car to commute to work. This was a materialistic age.

With the advent of television came such creations as the TV-top ornaments to decorate the television, as if it were another piece of furniture in the house. The TV dinner, a frozen three course meal, was another new phenomenon which succeeded in ending family discussions in most cases, so that the family could watch famous sitcoms. The television was one of the new influences on the family in the fifties.

Not only were the items from the era lighthearted and readily available, they were also well-designed in many cases. Products were no longer purely functional, but originality contributed to design with different colors and styles. Round forms went out of fashion as a visual style, so appliances became squarer, or "sheer," as they were called at the time.

4 Close-up of three Jensen tile wall hangings.

5 Porcelain wall planter in shape of a fish.

6 Squiggle vase, hand made by West Virginia glass, Weston, West Virginia.

7 Vase with pink and grey fish motif, unsigned.

A fresh imagery based on abstraction and science began to proliferate walls, windows, and metal-legged couches. Abstract design embodied the light spirit of the 1950s. Contemporary-looking, the new designs were sure to catch people's attention. Although the general public had a certain disdain for modern art, in the forms of cubism and abstraction in the halls of museums, ironically they sought abstract design for their home environment. The imagery of science and forward motion was prominent in the innovative shapes of furniture and colorful designs of formica countertops.

Fashions and decorations of the fifties inspired home decorating in full force. Americans embraced the modern look and rushed to fill their homes with items screaming as icons of innovation. Nothing could slip by the influences of the decade, evident even in furniture, interior decorations, even dish and glasswear. Pink and black were the favored colors with squiggles and atomic prints to give a sense of the "modern." The cocktail hour was more popular than ever before and evident in almost every household with trays designed for seltzer bottles, funky swizzle sticks, and tablecloths decorated with images of cocktail glasses.

8 An abstract shaped bowl with two candle holders. The color pink with grey crackles throughout are prominent designs from the fifties.

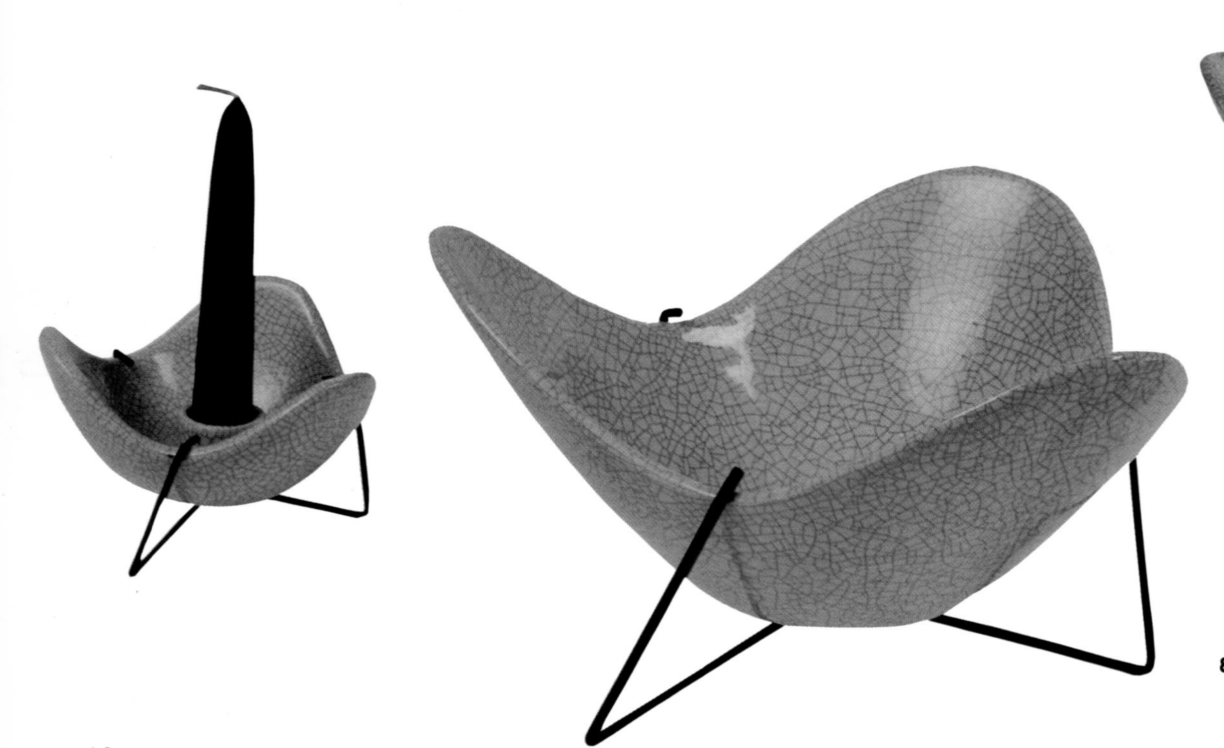

8

9

IN THE KITCHEN

A popular dinnerware from the fifties came from Red Wing, Minnesota. Although the Red Wing Pottery company began producing chinaware in 1935, its Red Wing china was most popular throughout the 1950s. The set of dishes pictured is known as "Fantasy." This pattern was advertised in the fifties as "our answer to those who 'love modern but simply can't live with it'." The pattern is hand painted in simple, broad strokes with a soft rose overglaze, giving the appropriate "modern" touch. The shapes took on delicate abstract floral forms which allowed the decorator to partake in the modern style of the decade without overdoing it.

Many pieces of Red Wing chinaware were hand decorated, and some were very complex. For example, the Tampico pattern used over 150 brushstrokes on the design. The most common patterns were sold for many years after being introduced. Examples of such patterns include the Concord, Anniversary and Futura patterns which were sold for ten to twelve years after they were first introduced. Other patterns were quite rare and saw limited production, for instance: White & Turquoise; Harvest; Bud; Nassau; and Labriego.

10

9 "Roselane Pasadena California." Aqua chinawear with blue lines and fish and ducks throughout. Shown here from set are a vase, coffee pot, salt & pepper shaker, platter, ashtrays and serving piece with wooden spoon. The Japanese influence is quite apparent here.

10 Pink Red Wing china dishes. "Red Wing hand painted." They display an interesting abstract design andtypical fifties color. Part of set.

11 Palm tree dishwear. "Tahiti by Continental Kilns, Underglaze, hand painted. USA." Shown here are the platter, plate, butter plate, and cup and saucer.

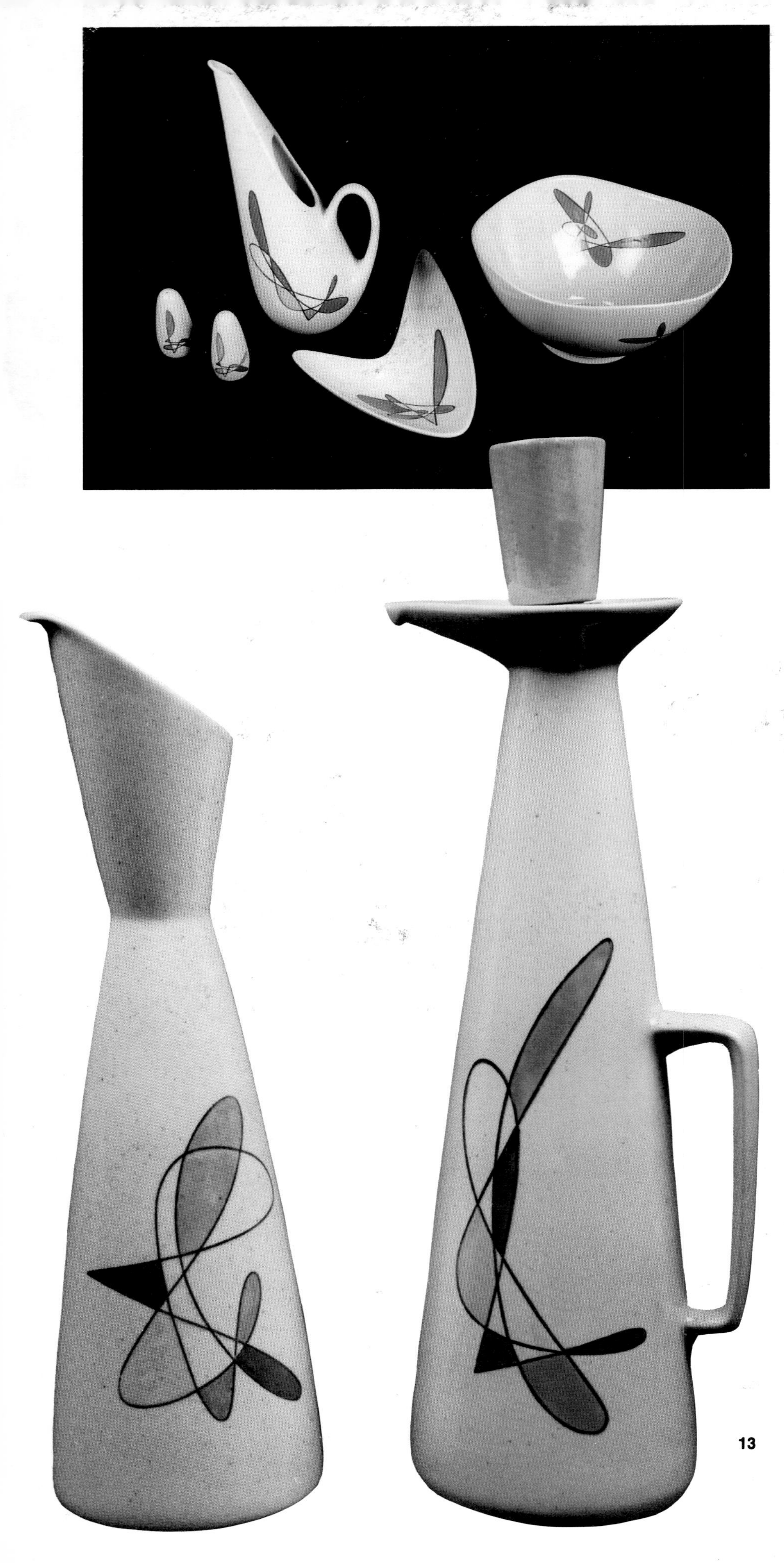

12

The Red Wing dinnerware was sold through a variety of markets, including department stores, jewelry stores and other retail establishments. The Potteries themselves also had retail outlets. The Red Wing Pottery closed in 1967 after having made patterns for thirty-two years.

The kitchen exhibited a broad expanse of themes common in the fifties, from harlequins, to the circus, cowboys, Hawaii, and abstract expressionism. As new appliances emerged, the kitchen's decor had to match, with fabulous modern patterns on china and glassware as well as interesting prints on tablecloths and other linens.

13

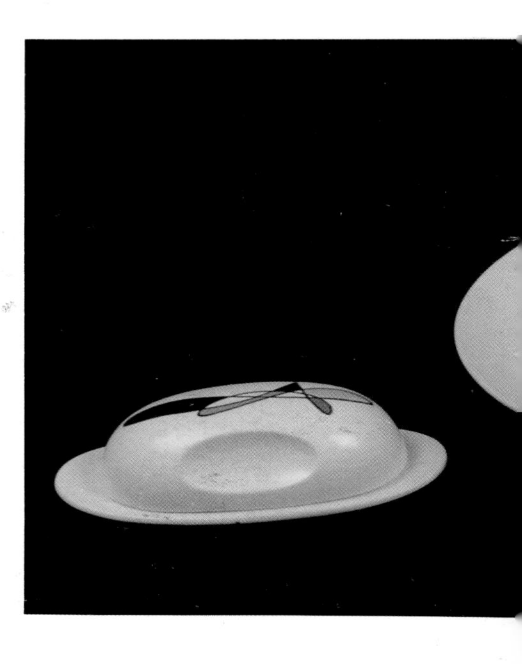

14

15

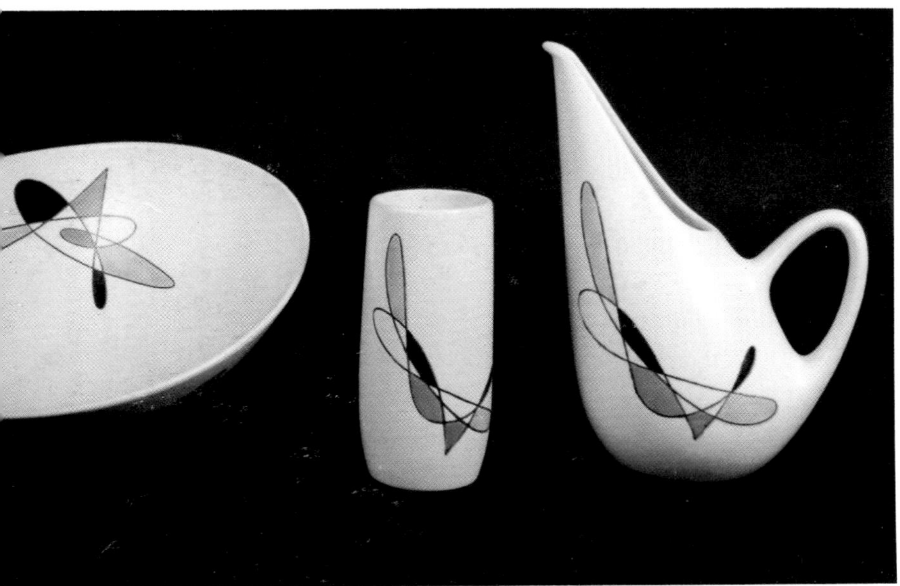

16

12 Poppytrail set: salt and pepper, bowl 12" diam., pitcher, and dish, all in the "California Freeform" design. This particular pattern was produced during the latter half of the 1950s. Its flowing lines and boomerang forms indicate a touch of Kandinsky or Miro. Comes in three different color combinations by Metlox.

13 Two decanters in the "California Freeform" poppytrail pattern.

14 More "California Freeform" dishware from Poppytrail, with the "Made in California" seal.

15 Poppytrail chinawear, "Aztec" design, an American Indian motif. White with black design. 8" plate.

16 Poppytrail bowl, butter dish, pitcher and vase or glass, again in "California Freeform."

17

18

19

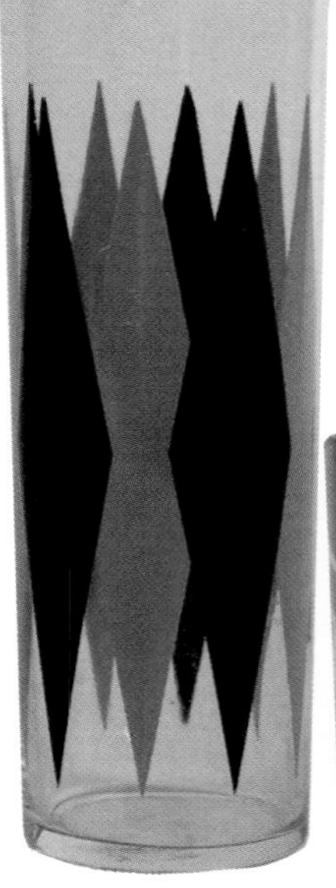

20

21

22

23

17 Small pink glass which reads "gaité" with a bird in a heart cage.

18 Black and blue glass with a black squiggle. Squiggles were a common fifties design.

19 Merry-go-round carousel motif on a frosted glass.

20 Harlequin diamonds in pink and black, couldn't get much more fifties on this glass, 7".

21 Black and gold with African figure on glass.

22 Whimsical flamingo glass.

23 "Girlie" glass made of pottery.

30

29

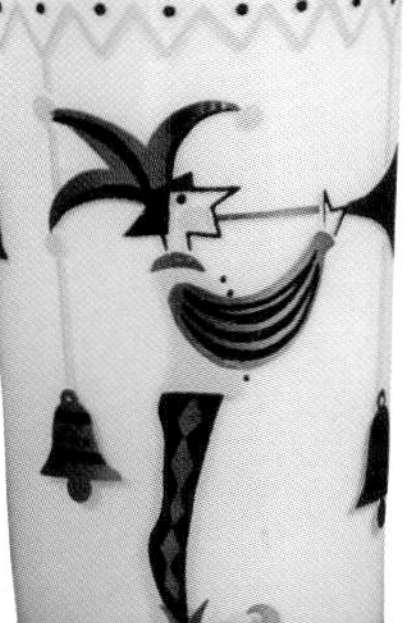

28

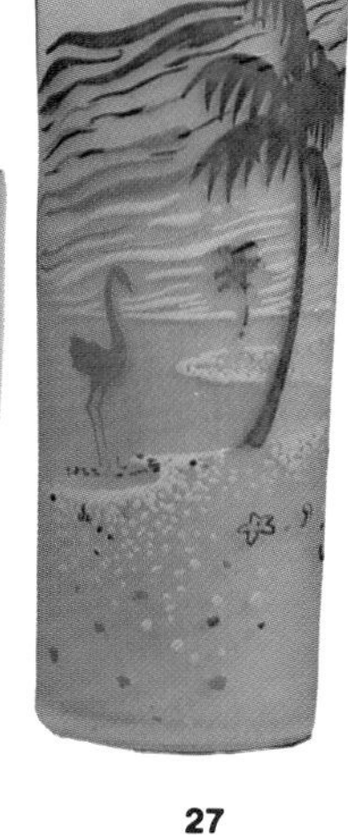

27

26

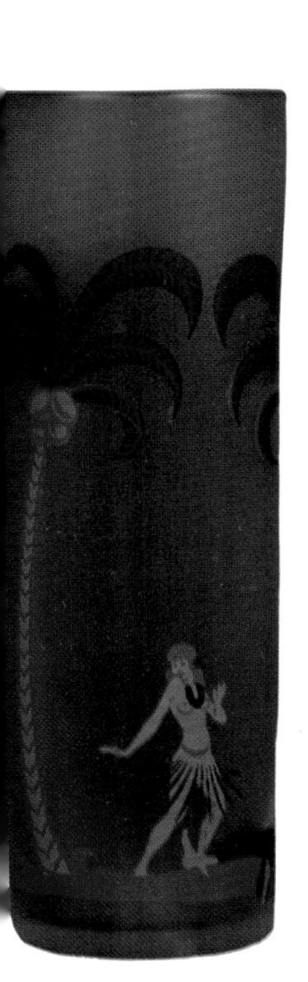

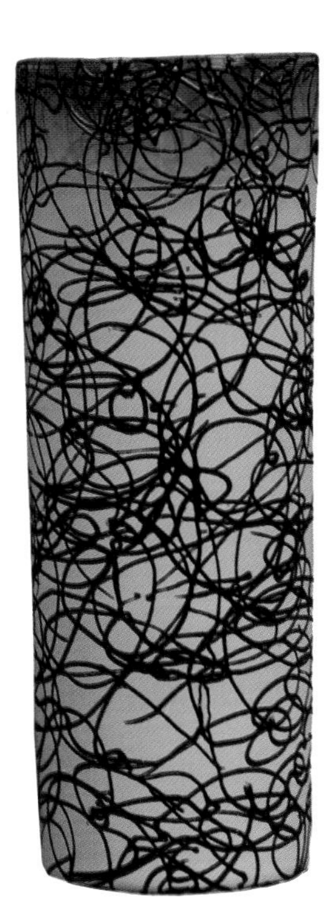

25

24

24 Frosted Hawaiian motif glass.

25 Pink & black squiggle pattern on iced tea glass.

26 Fishing lures glass, with black gold and polychrome.

27 Flamingo and palm tree frosted iced tea glass.

28 Frosted glass with harlequin.

29 Rooster glass, black and gold, copyright by Fred Press.

30 White zebra glass.

All glasses, sets of 6.

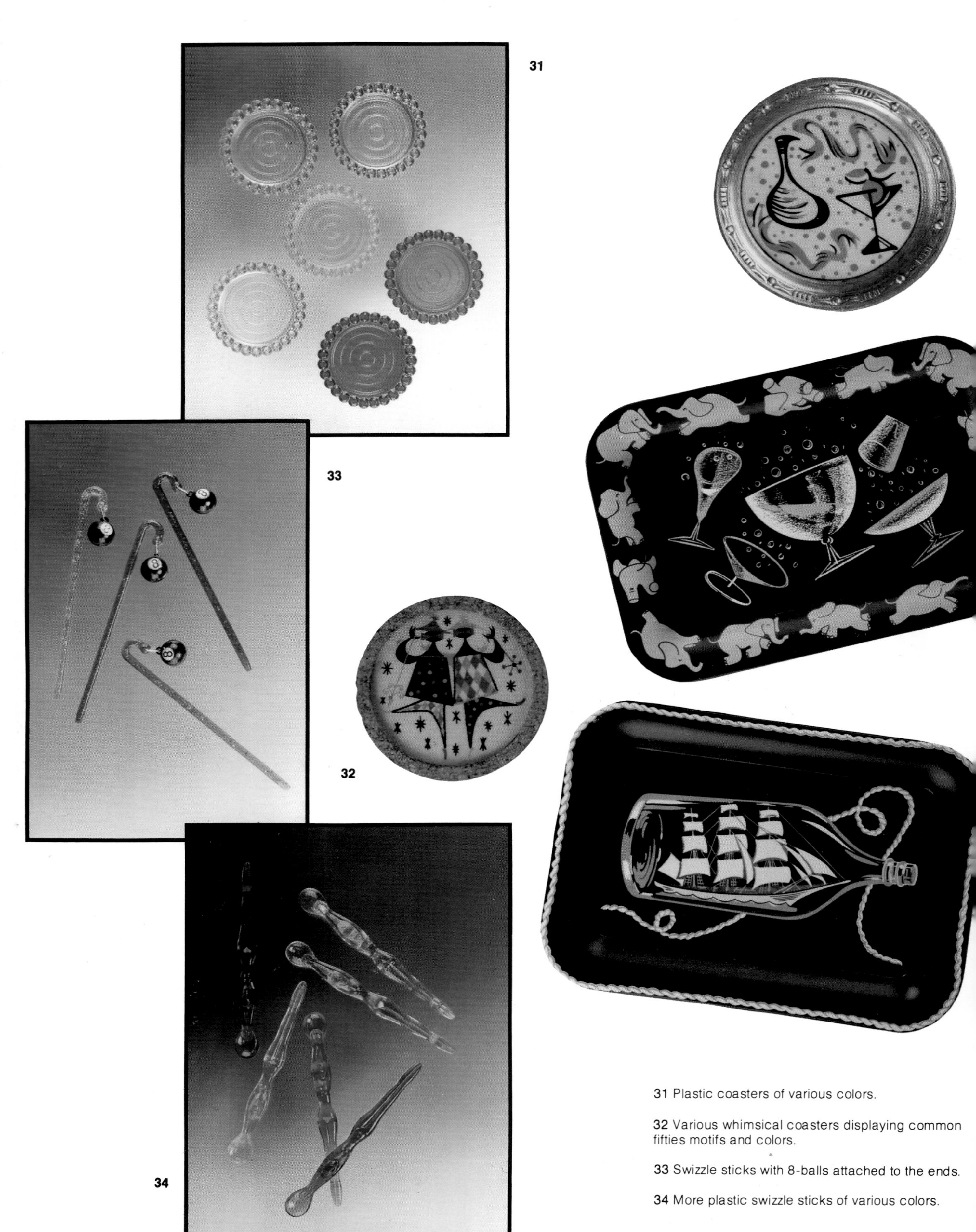

31 Plastic coasters of various colors.

32 Various whimsical coasters displaying common fifties motifs and colors.

33 Swizzle sticks with 8-balls attached to the ends.

34 More plastic swizzle sticks of various colors.

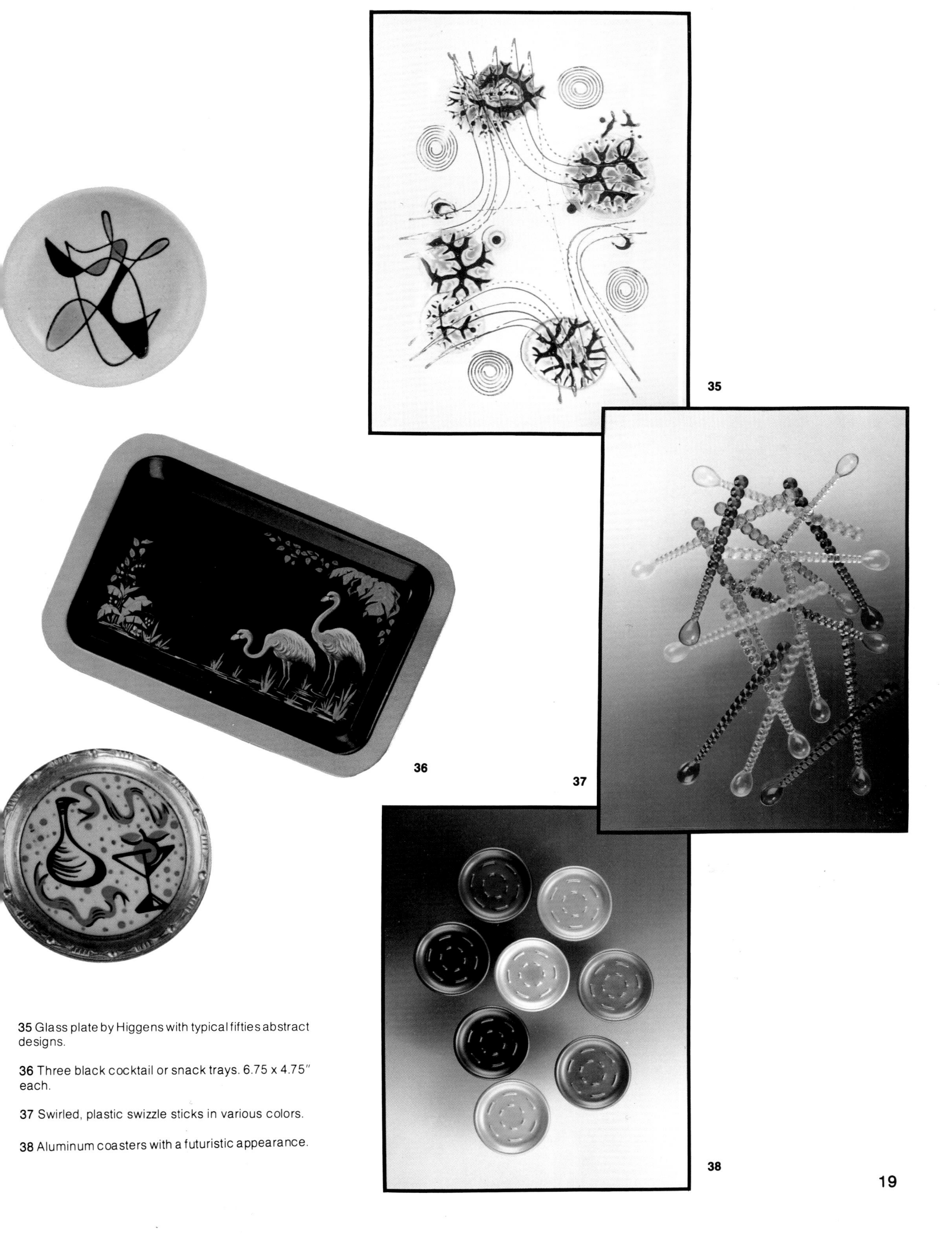

35

36

37

38

35 Glass plate by Higgens with typical fifties abstract designs.

36 Three black cocktail or snack trays. 6.75 x 4.75″ each.

37 Swirled, plastic swizzle sticks in various colors.

38 Aluminum coasters with a futuristic appearance.

39

39 Round, formica pedestal table with vinyl covered chairs. The vinyl on the chairs is signed and dated 1958. The curtains are fiberglass with abstract airplanes.

40 Fifties blue with black and pink with black, cookware in a squiggle pattern. Enamel and granitewear.

41 Wonderful ice bucket with a very abstract design. 7" x 7.25" diam.

42 Not only is the pattern very fifties, but the colors make this piece even more incredible, pink and black squiggle punch bowl.

40

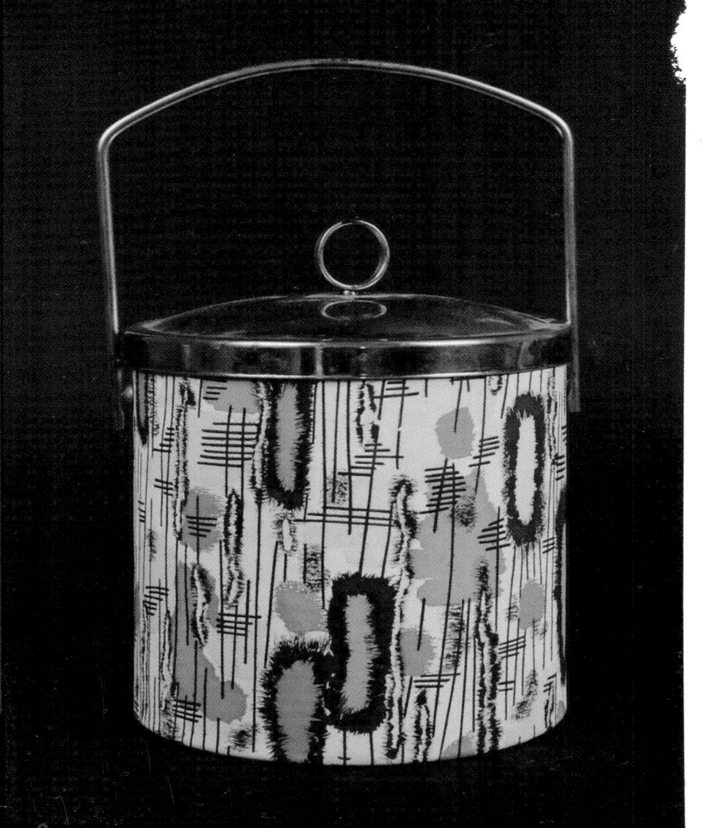
41

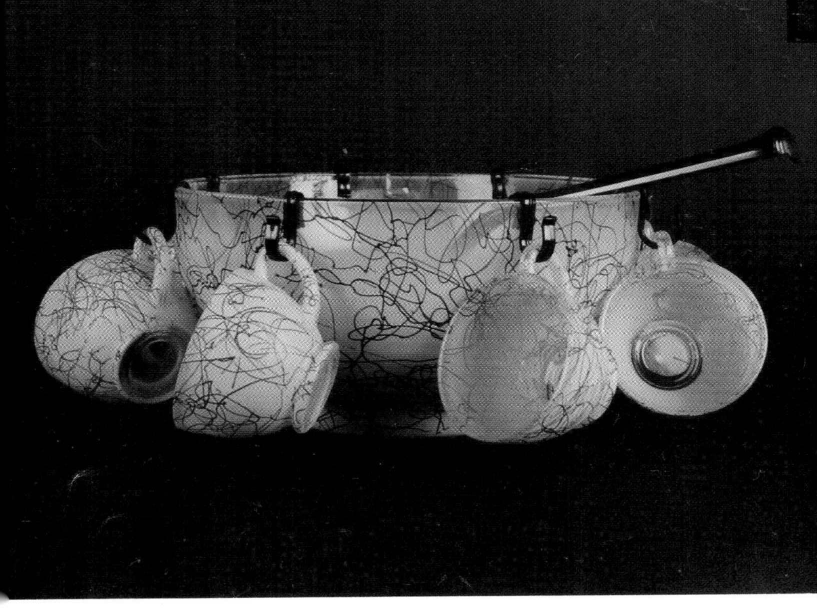
42

43 Linen dinner napkins with dance figures or spear bearers, an abstract yet primitive design.

44 Hand towel with cocktail design by "Leacock Prints." "2 ounces for men, 1 ounce for ladies."

45 White tablecloth with a cocktail design.

46 Five cocktail napkins, each with a different woman's portrait, very "cheesecaky."

46

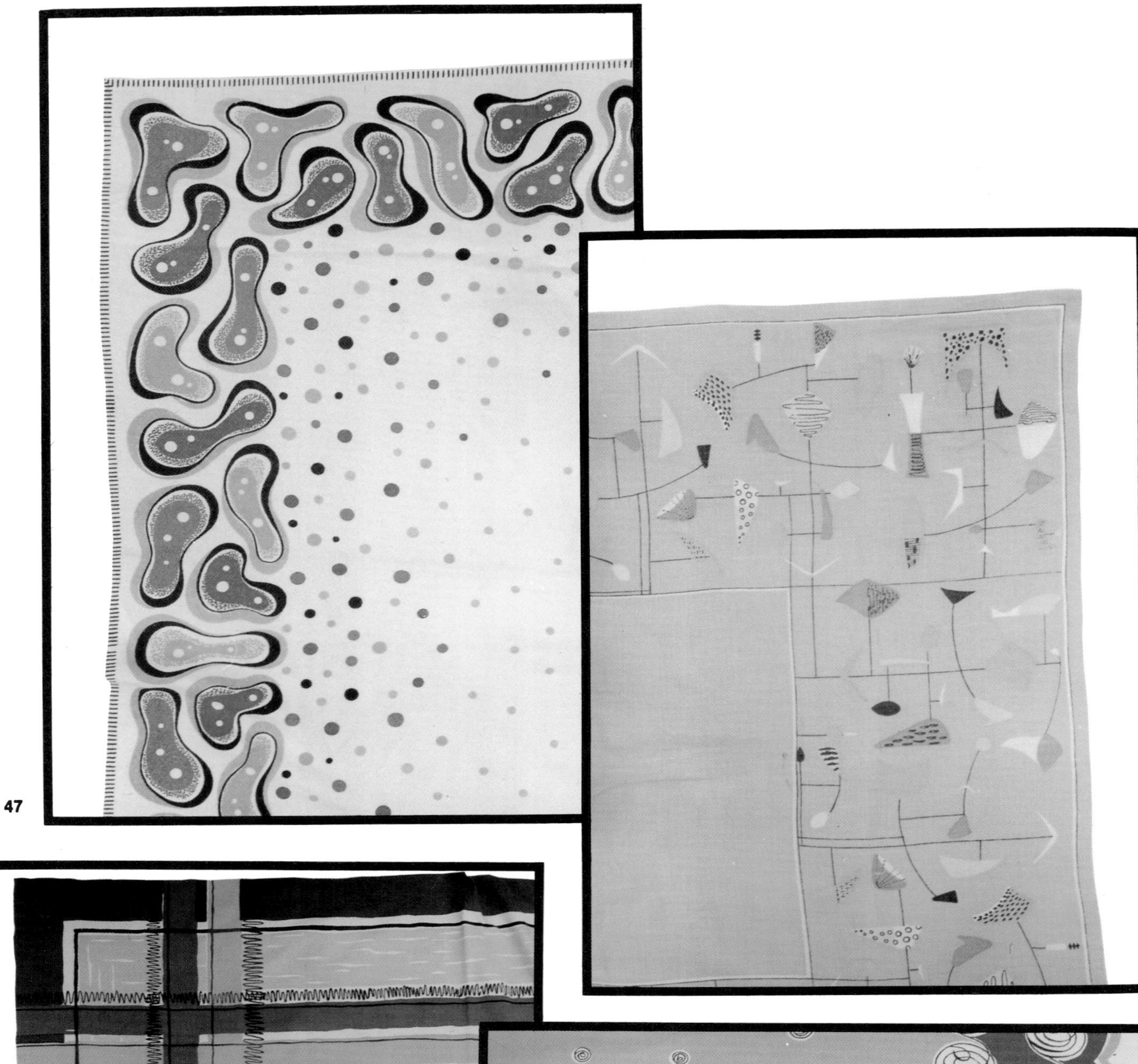

47

48

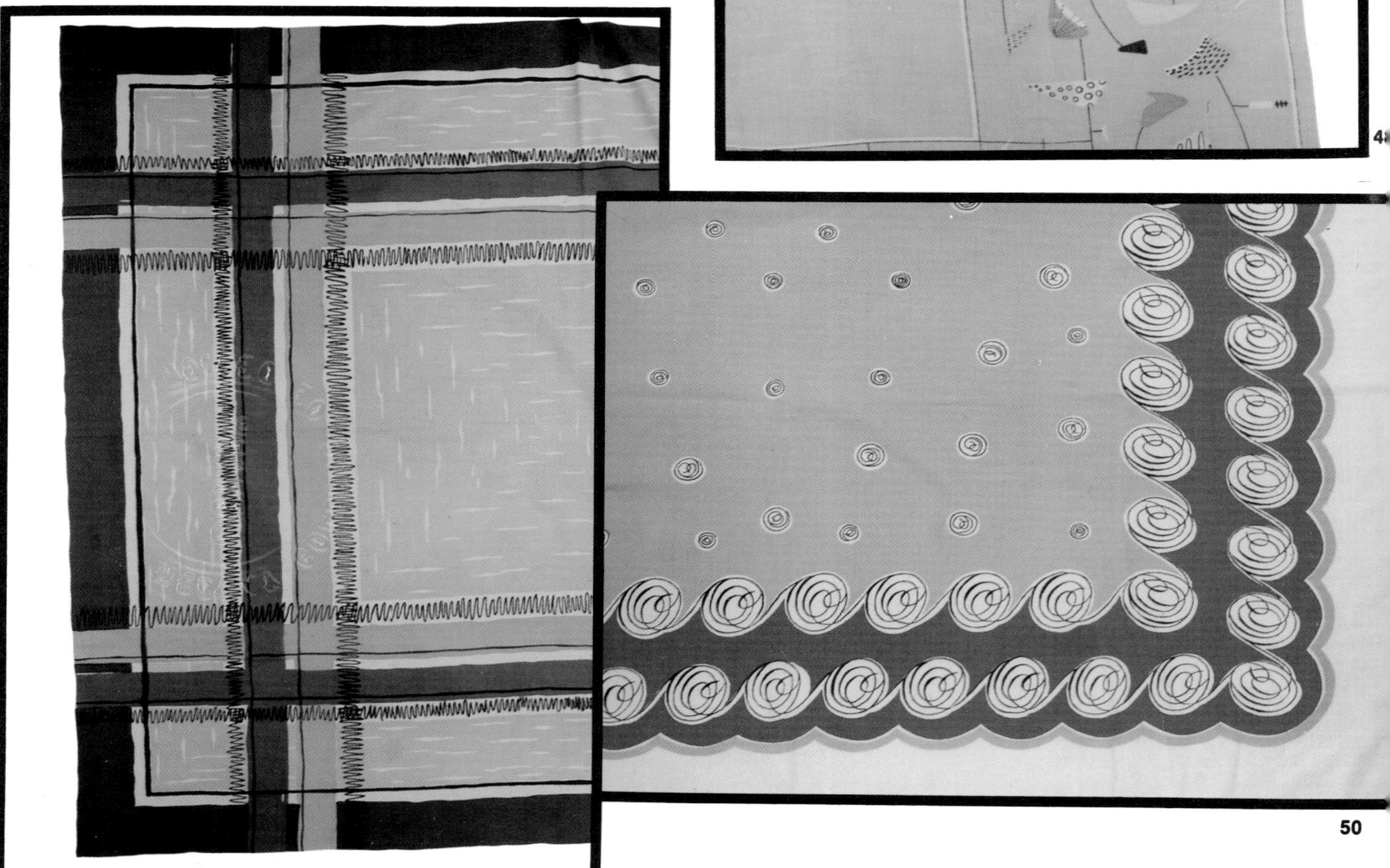

49

50

51

47 Tablecloth with funny abstract ameoboid-type shapes or footprints, depending on your perspective. The colors and design are very 1950s.

48 Wonderful 1950s tablecloth with chartreuse center and Calderesque mobile design around the border.

49 Geometric tablecloth with green, pink, and yellow. No label. The squiggles remind one of a Modriani design.

50 Grey, white and red tablecloth with squiggles along the border and throughout.

51 Cocktail glasses printed on this tray entice the user with a shadowed effect.

52 Black tray by "Milito" displaying cocktail decanters in a Picasso-esque design.

53 Black and white, square metal tray with dogs and cocktail glasses. "Social Supper Trays." Artist, "C.P.M." 13.25" square.

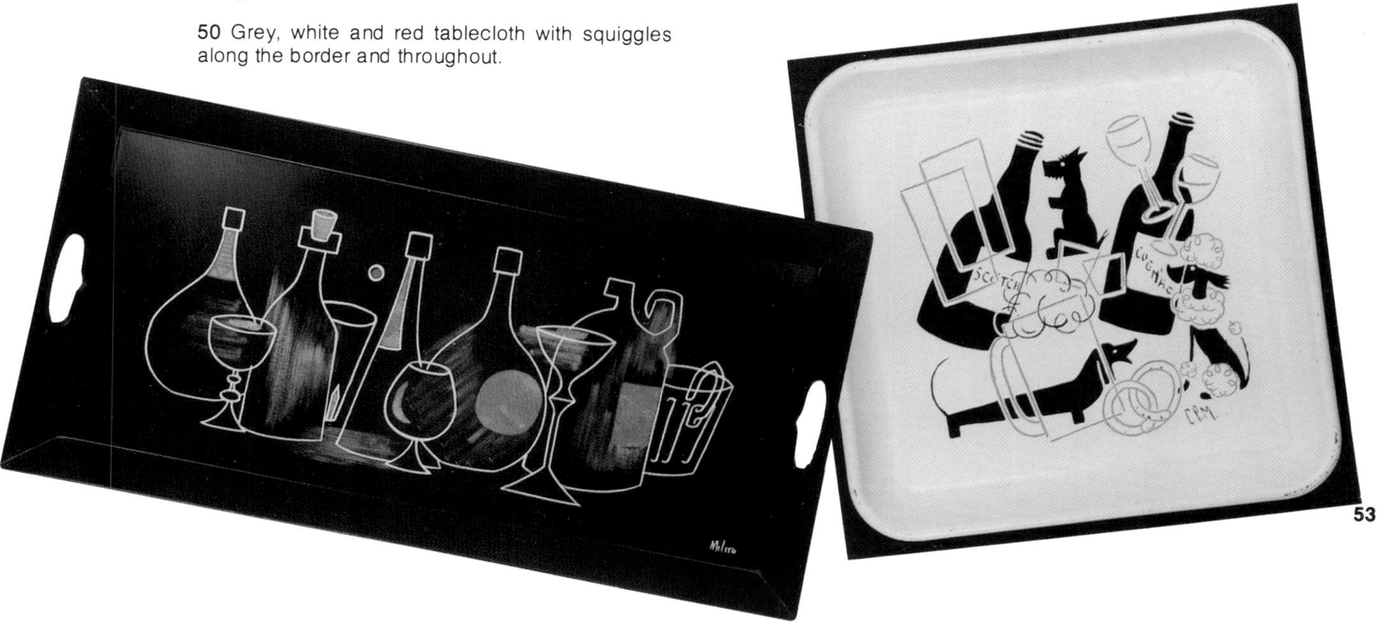

53

What's my Line?
Who Said That?
Strike It Rich
Studio One
Show of Shows
Mr. Peepers
Suspense
T-V Playhouse
I Love Lucy
Playhouse of Stars
Life With Father
Comedy Hour
Name's the Same
Dragnet

54

What's my Line?
Who Said That?
Strike It Rich
Studio One
Show of Shows
Mr. Peepers
Suspense
T-V Playhouse
I Love Lucy
Playhouse of Stars
Life With Father
Comedy Hour
Name's the Same
Dragnet

54 Two metal trays in black and pink with comedy and tragedy masks surrounded by many popular television program lines from the fifties. "The Comedy Hour." 17.5".

55 Lightweight metal tray with woman in tan, somewhat like a ballerina.

56 Broncking cowboy on bull on a bright orange tray with white border. "Hopper." 17.5".

57 Fish pattern tray.

58 Circus tray "The Greatest Show on Earth, Paramount Pictures." 17.5".

59 "Reach for the Rhythm" red musical tray with silhouetted figures playing jazz. 17.5".

60 Shakespearean tragedy and comedy masks. "Couroc of Monterey, California."

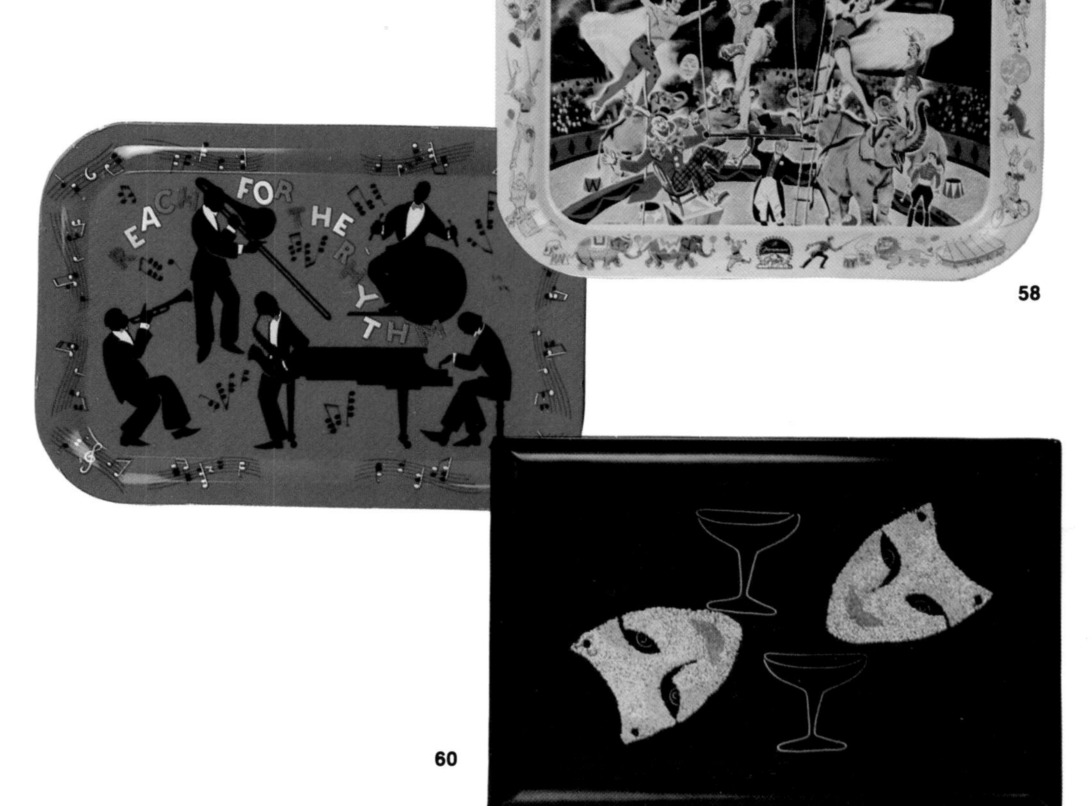

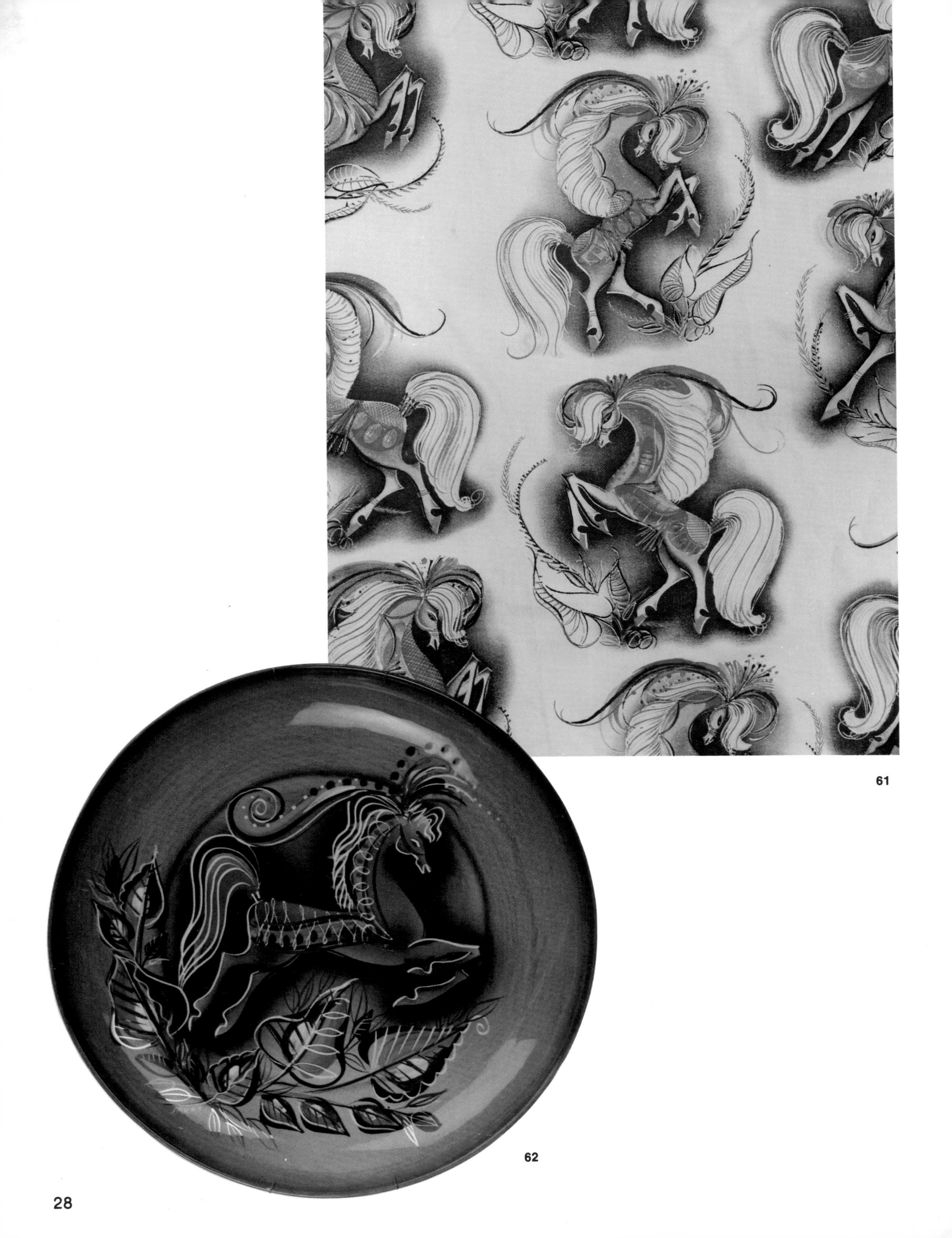

61

62

63

ART POTTERY

Art pottery took on a very different attitude from the other mass-produced items of the 1950s. Opposed to the abstractionism and the machine technology, it held a simplicity and purity that stood in contrast to the growing complexity and rampant consumerism of American life at the time. Art pottery stood in contrast to the designs of New York School artists of abstract design and the modern designs of futuristic architects and designers of mass production. This was a hard time for the craftsperson.

Sascha Brastoff is one of the most well-known and successful of the art potters. Born in Cleveland, Ohio in 1918, he exhibited his creativity at the Cleveland School of Art and Cleveland Ballet in the 1930s. His sculptures were exhibited at the Syracuse Museum before he was twenty years old.

Ceramics was simply a hobby for him, until, in the late 1940s he attracted the attention of many Hollywood stars. Through the patronage of financier Winthrop Rockefeller, he was able to start his own ceramics business in Los Angeles which lasted from 1947 through 1963.

Although he created steel sculptures and kept at his hobby as a gold and jewel-smith, his focus was on ceramic design. After his original building was burned to ruins in 1952, a new ceramic studio was built and its design was awarded by the American Institute of Architects. Thousands of visitors annually were welcomed to these studios to see the exhibits and watch the artists as they worked.

In the beginning, Sascha signed all his pieces "Sascha Brastoff," as they were all unique pieces made personally by him. Later, they were signed "Sascha B." and were made in part by studio artists in his factory. Still later, as the factory grew, he created his identifying rooster decals and signed the pieces "Sascha Brastoff California USA" or "Sascha Brastoff Fine China California." The decals were applied under the final glaze as an additional identifying mark.

Sascha ceramics are well-known for their free-flowing, rhythmic style, usually with a rooster or flying horse motif. Often he used a glaze and reintroduced the ancient techniques of sgraffito. Sgraffito is the process by which a design is incised with a sharp tool into wet clay.

64

61 Sascha Brastoff moved into designing fabrics, and wonderfully so. Sascha horse pattern on this fabric.

62 Sascha plate made of porcelain with a sharp and colorful image of the jumping horse. 15.5 diameter.

63 Another plate with a pink horse, signed "Sascha B." 15.25" diameter.

64 A square tile by Sasha, designed with one of his jumping horses.

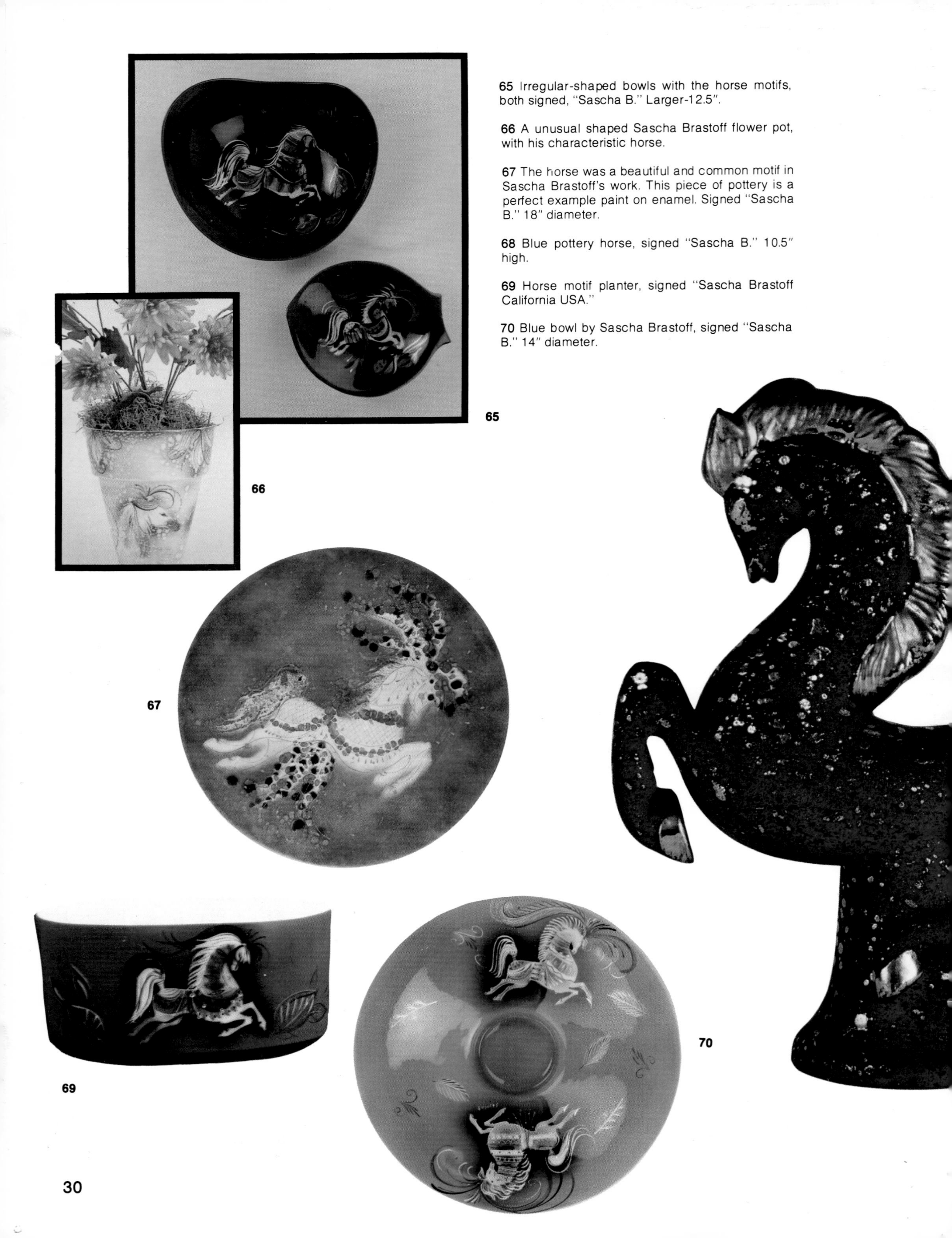

65 Irregular-shaped bowls with the horse motifs, both signed, "Sascha B." Larger-12.5".

66 A unusual shaped Sascha Brastoff flower pot, with his characteristic horse.

67 The horse was a beautiful and common motif in Sascha Brastoff's work. This piece of pottery is a perfect example paint on enamel. Signed "Sascha B." 18" diameter.

68 Blue pottery horse, signed "Sascha B." 10.5" high.

69 Horse motif planter, signed "Sascha Brastoff California USA."

70 Blue bowl by Sascha Brastoff, signed "Sascha B." 14" diameter.

65

66

67

69

70

71

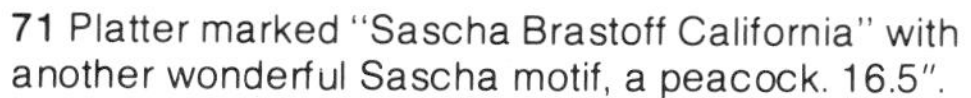

71 Platter marked "Sascha Brastoff California" with another wonderful Sascha motif, a peacock. 16.5".

72

72 Tall, Sascha Brastoff vase with a peacock motif, 20" high.

73 Ceramic bird wall decorations, by Sascha Brastoff.

74 A white rooster plate by Sascha Brastoff, 11.75" with a full signature.

He sometimes applied gold under one of the final glazes. Many of his designs could be obtained only with four separate firings and washing or spraying the cover glaze gave a speckled effect. Each piece is unique as the Brastoff artists follow a theme, not a pattern.

When Pablo Picasso started work in ceramics as a new medium in 1947, his primitive motifs and figural designs influenced many other artists. The primitive designs were important new themes in the 1950s.

68

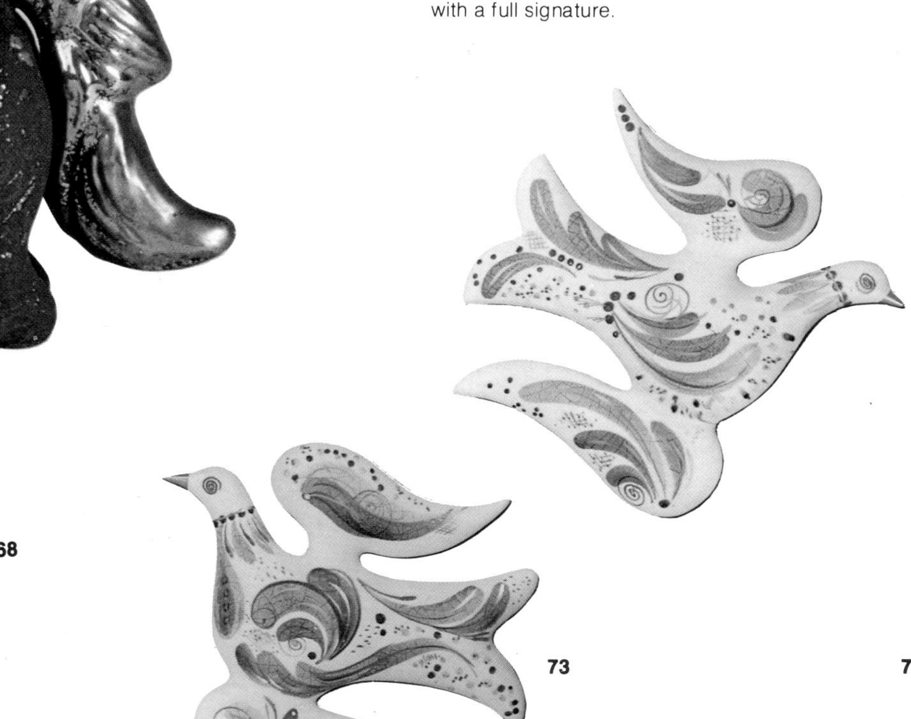

73

74

75 Sascha Brastoff fabric, grey with shading. This particular pattern is called, "Ballerina."

76 Sascha tile depicting a common fifties motif: a mermaid. Signed, "Sascha."

77 Statue of African woman with bowl on head. "Sascha B." 19.75"

78 Plate with interesting Egyptian-type figures. Marked, "Sascha Brastoff." 12.25" diameter.

79 Sascha pitcher in shape of primitive woman. 13" high.

80 Large platter with Southwestern motif, by Sascha Brastoff. 19" diameter.

81 Sascha rooster, original piece made by him, signed original. Wire.

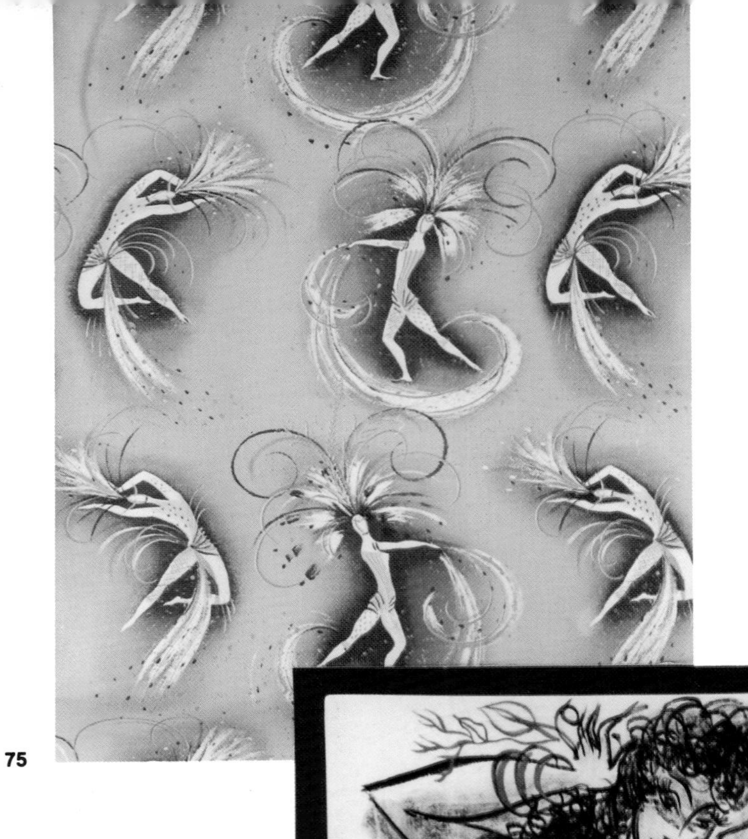

75

76

77

78

79

80

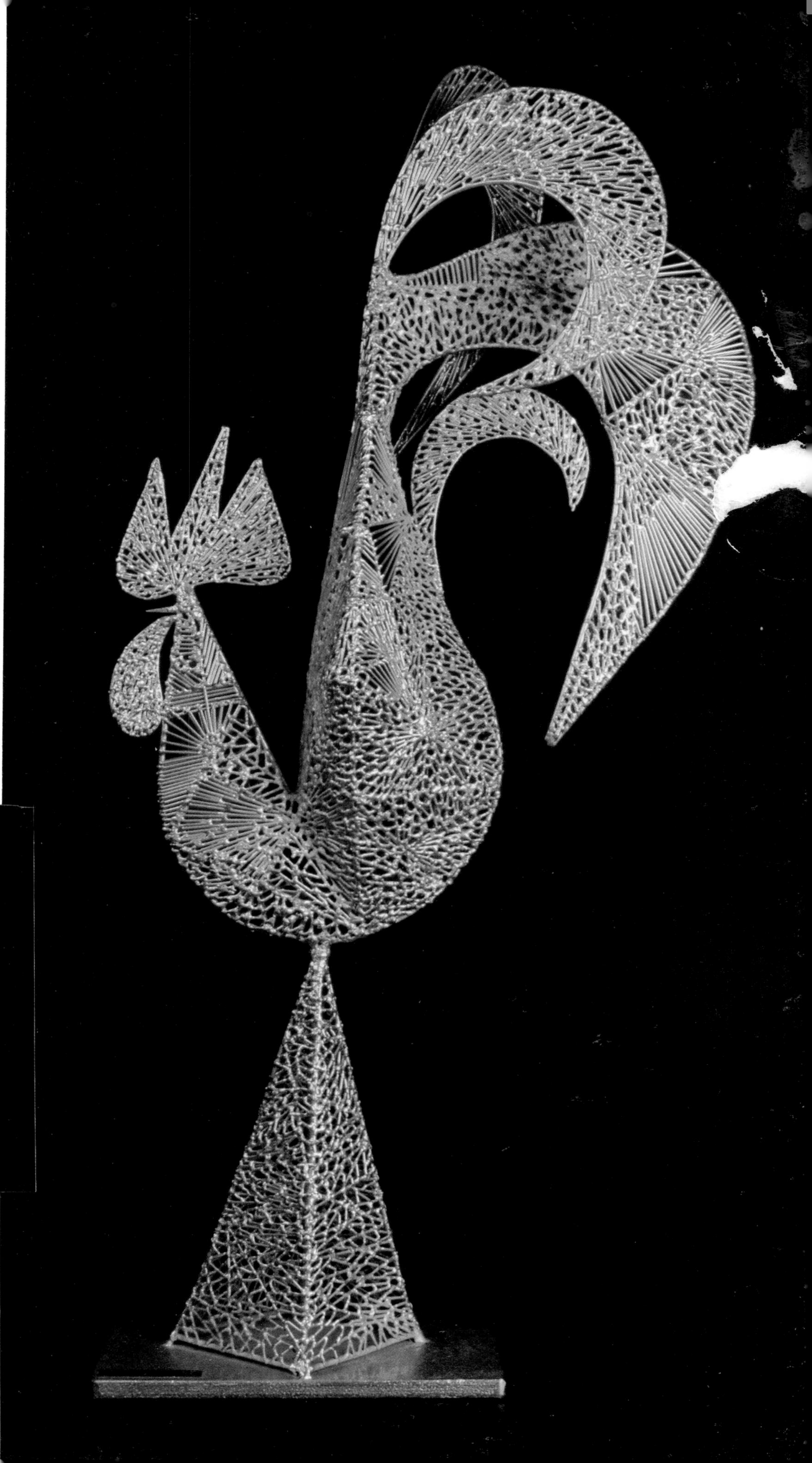

81

82

83

84

82 Sascha Brastoff mugs with fish decorating the front side.

83 Original chalk painting of fish by Sascha Brastoff.

84 Wonderful Sascha Brastoff fish tile, signed "Sascha B."

85 Sascha dish, spiritual motif with a gossamer. Large platter, 17.75" x 13.5".

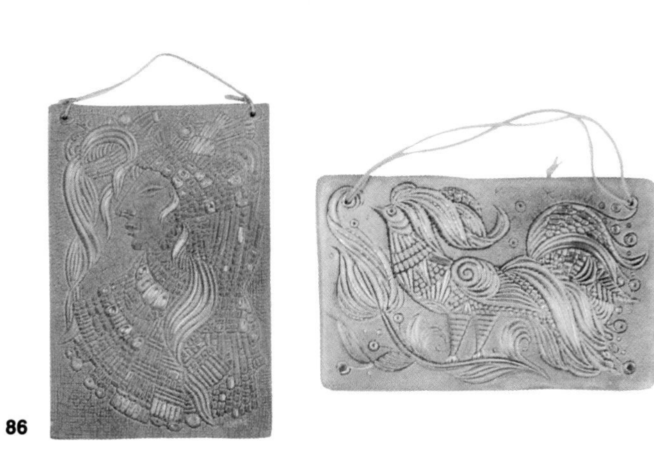

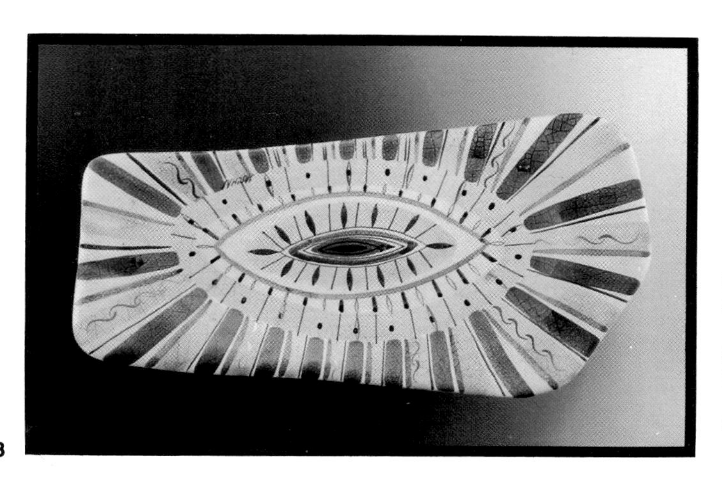

86 Two clay wall hangings with sgraffito, one of a rooster and the other of an Ancient Egyptian person.

87 Profile of Indian headress using the sgraffito process on a large platter.

88 Sascha Brastoff dish with abstract stripe pattern.

89

89 Set of plates with folk dancers by Sascha Brastoff. 10″ diameter.

90 Sascha vase with house motif. 11″ x 9.5″.

91 Sascha plate, all ceramic. Signed, "Sascha Brastoff." Dated, '55. The Sascha Brastoff signature means this piece was made specifically by Sascha himself, as opposed to one of his studio potters.

92 Sascha Brastoff plate set of cupid statue.

93 "Sascha B." signed plate from a whole set. Barn with a rooster on top with yellow border.

94 Enamel plate signed, "Sascha B."

90

91

92

93

94

95 Sascha Brastoff coffee pot, signed "Sascha B." 15.5" high.

96 One of a large set of fruit plates, each different, by Sascha Brastoff.

97 Sascha Brastoff large, square platter, signed "Sascha B." 14.75".

98 A signed Sascha Brastoff rooster. 23" high.

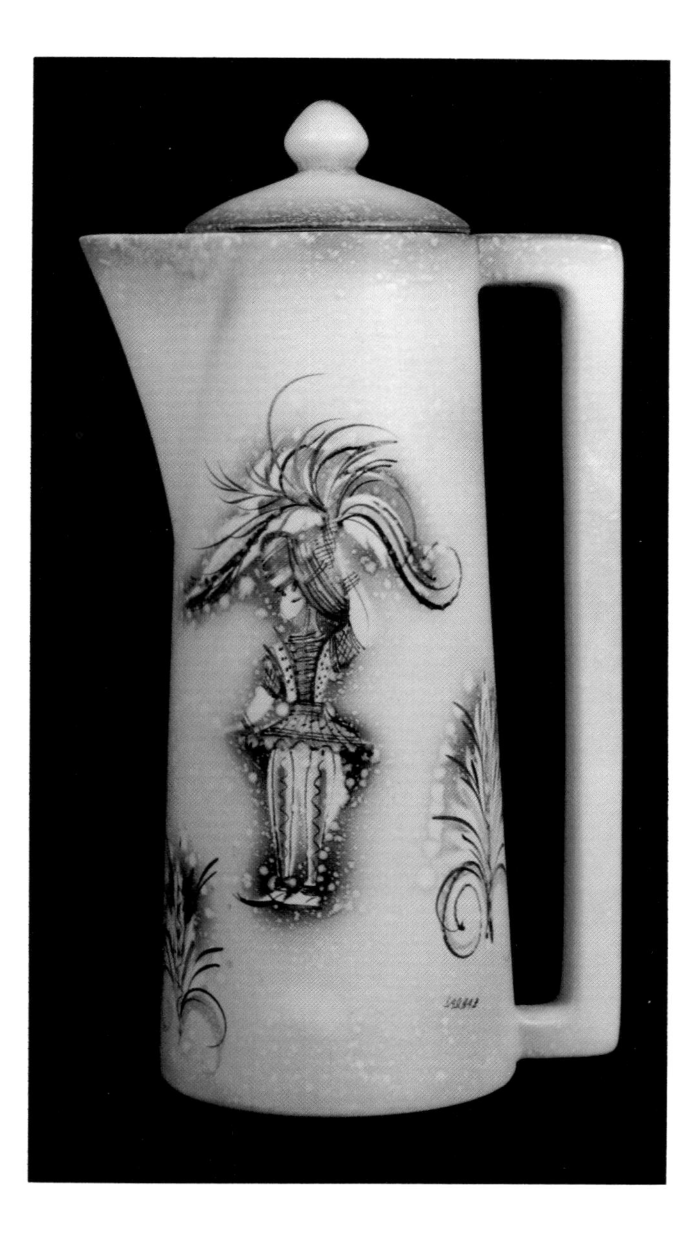

95

96

97

98

HOUSEHOLD FURNISHINGS

The furnishings for the homes of this period have a distinct look. With new materials such as formica, vinyl and other synthetic fibers, a faddish and modern look was obtainable for the home. Tubular steel and wire furniture was "the popular look" of the time. A preoccupation with the future and popular science was also reflected readily in the furniture. The popular starburst light fixture shown here is a good example of the public's craze for science technology and space research. The fixture's design reminds one of the images of atoms and neutrons in chemistry.

Faith in abstraction for the fine and applied arts brought these two disciplines closer together than ever before as is evident in furniture designs. In the 1930s, the modern movement claimed that "form follow function." In the post-modern era of the 1950s, the idea was that function need not be threatened by a more adventurous expression of form. Abstract expressionist design did not neccessarily displace function.

Shapes were softer and more organic, in contrast to previous styles. Furniture design carried the concept of curvilinear and the abstract. The curved sofa

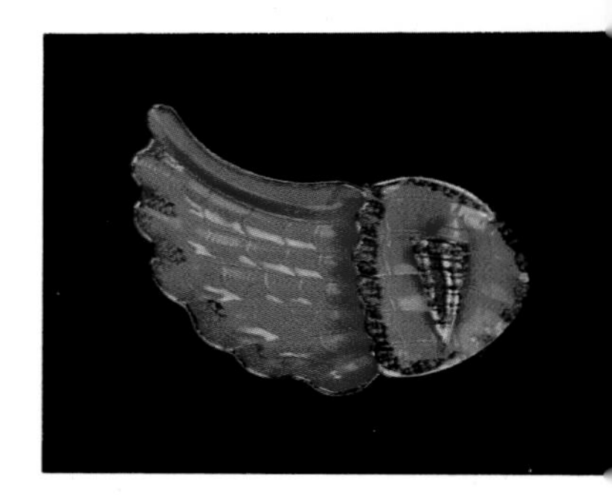

101

99 Seashells go pink and gold for this whimsical '50s ashtray.

100 1950s living room with amoeba-shaped table and fifties fabric on the atomic-shaped sofa. A Moss Lamp Co. floor lamp sits behind the sofa...the top lights up, the base glows, and the figure spins!

101 Starburst fixture which sits above the formica kitchen table. A popular fixture in the fifties, calling to mind outer-space images of futuristic style.

102 An Italian ceramic of a cocktail party, a festive decoration for a 1950s sitting room.

103 A 1950s living room's pride and joy: Sylvania television set, producing, of course, a black and white picture.

pictured here has a wonderful abstract print, and the amoeba-shaped table fits well next to it. The television set was a prominent addition to the home and reached its maturity in the 1950s. Soon, almost every household had a television in its living room.

The artist's palette itself became a very common design in the 1950s, as is seen in the shapes of tables, ashtrays, and advertisements, to name a few. With the reopening of France after the war, the artist was once again encouraged to be 'Bohemian' "a person living an unconventional life usually in a colony with others" (Webster's Dictionary), and this was reflected in the thriving artist's center in New York City of Soho, and the emergence of the term 'beatniks' who beat the time of the new music, and otherwise "reject the mores of established society" (Webster's Dictionary).

102

100

103

Moss Lamps became well-known phenomena of the 1950s. Based in San Francisco, California, the company advertised its lamps in 1958 as "conversation pieces." They emphasized their "original designs, unique styling and fascinating combinations of textures and colors." Often using glitter in their bases and decorative columns, the lamps are typical of the "modern" look of the fifties.

A specialty of Moss Lamps are the figures which rest decoratively on stands and oftentimes spin by the flick of a switch. These special spinners are prizes with collectors today. A Moss Lamp in the living room setting, shown here for example, is a spinner lamp. Other lamps have music boxes in addition to the spinning figures, making them even more exceptional as true entertainment centers.

104

105

104 Ceramic atomic lamp. Grey, pink and white. 20.5".

105 Lamp with a squiggle abstract print and swirled effect.

106 Moss lamp with Hawaiian man sitting under a palm tree and a Hawaiian pattern lamp shade. Moss Lamp Co. 27" high.

106 The same Moss lamp with a Hawaiian woman. Moss Lamp Co.

107 Representative of the 50's fascination with the tropics, this "wild-style" lamp base has a native man dressed in leopard-skin poised to strike a gong.

108 A Moss lamp with glitter pillars and rock 'n roll star in the middle. Moss Lamp Co. The man spins, therefore, the lamp is called a spinner lamp. 50" high.

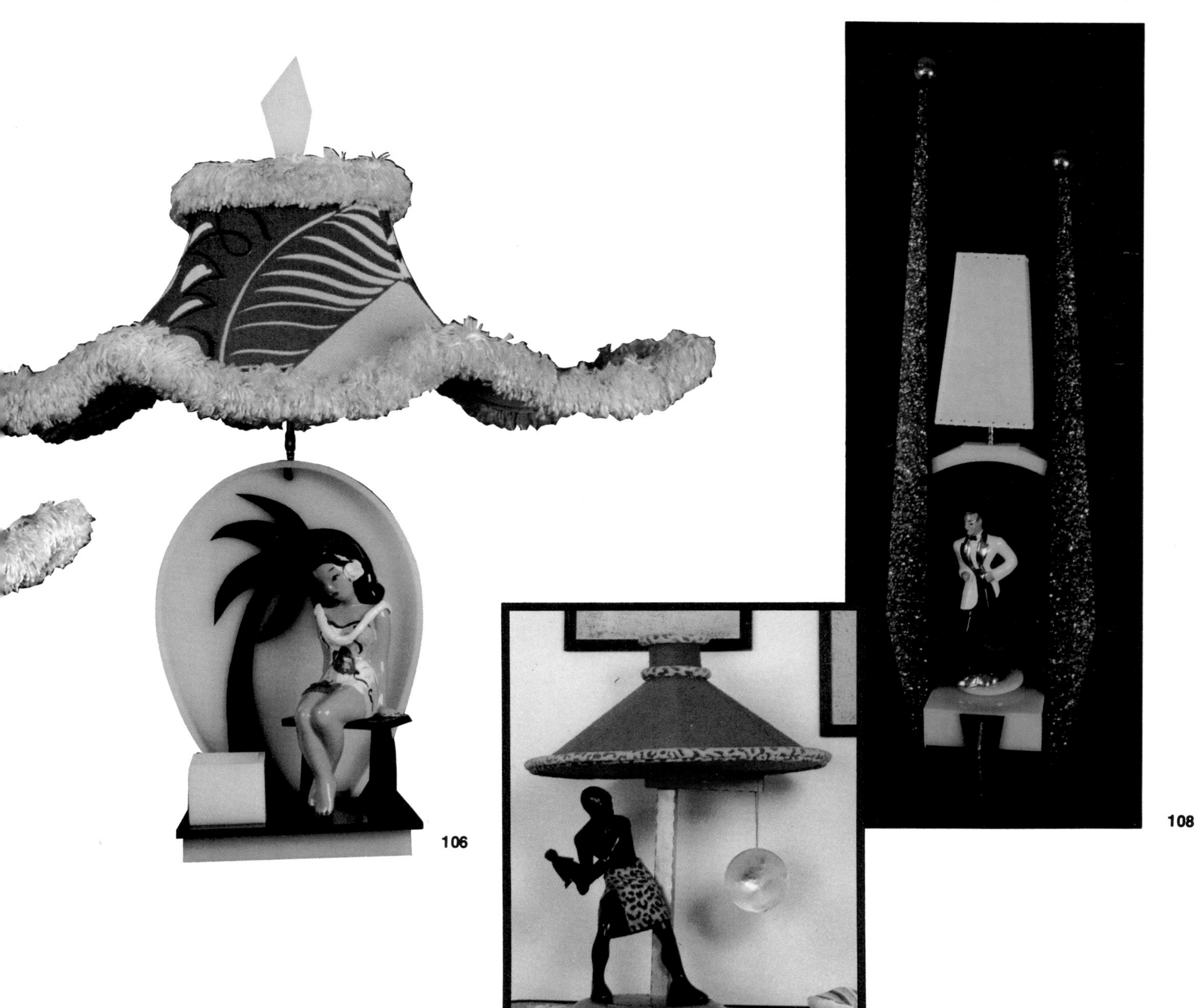

106

107

108

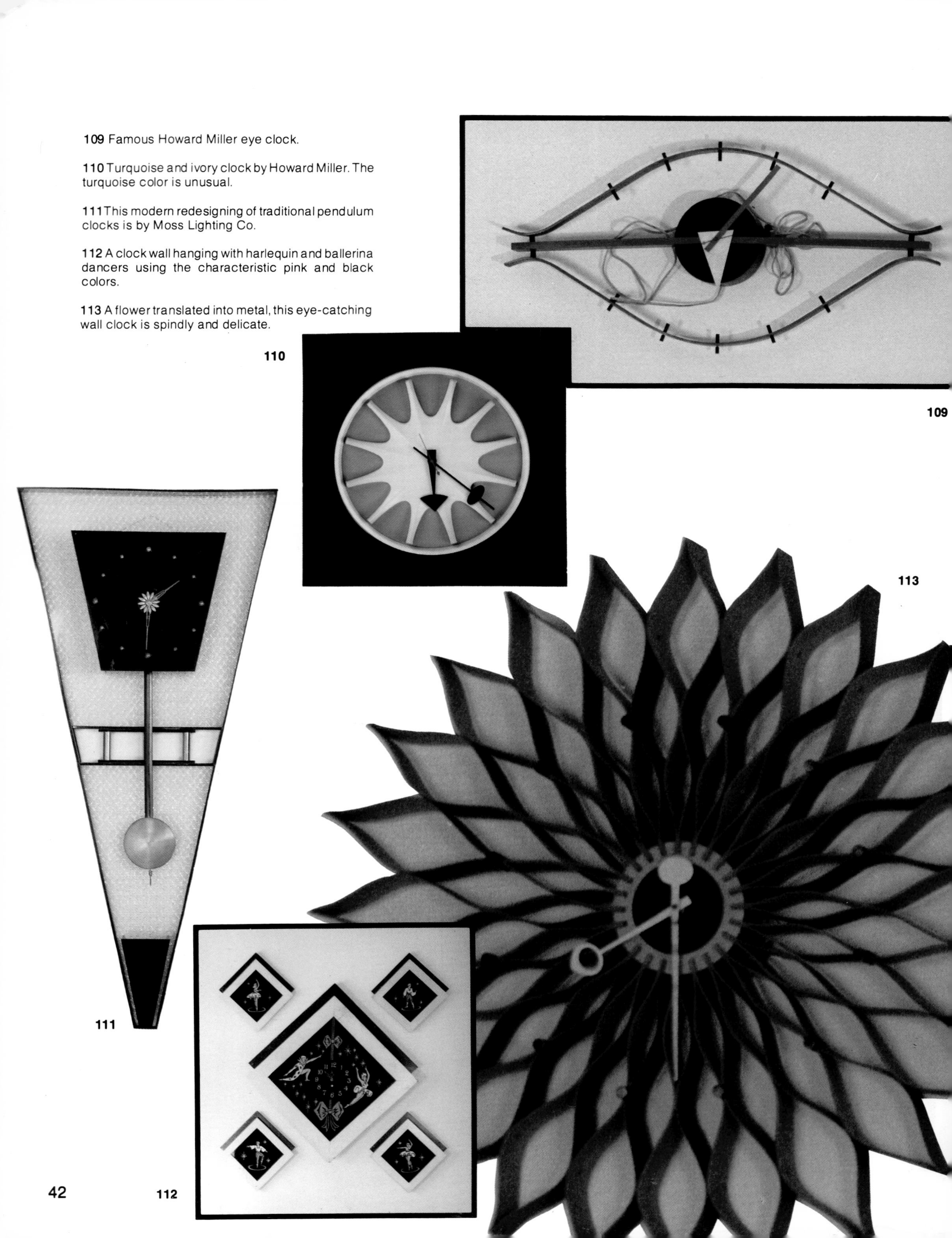

109 Famous Howard Miller eye clock.

110 Turquoise and ivory clock by Howard Miller. The turquoise color is unusual.

111 This modern redesigning of traditional pendulum clocks is by Moss Lighting Co.

112 A clock wall hanging with harlequin and ballerina dancers using the characteristic pink and black colors.

113 A flower translated into metal, this eye-catching wall clock is spindly and delicate.

110

109

113

111

112

114 Two wall hangings of ballerinas. Ballet was a ubiquitous motif of the 1950s. 17" x 8.75". Unknown artist. Plaster.

115 A 1940s painting, no signature. A great example of art kitsch.

116 Silvertone "Transistor, Twin speakers" radio with squiggle design on the front.

117 Wonderful fifties squiggle pattern on this 1950s chair.

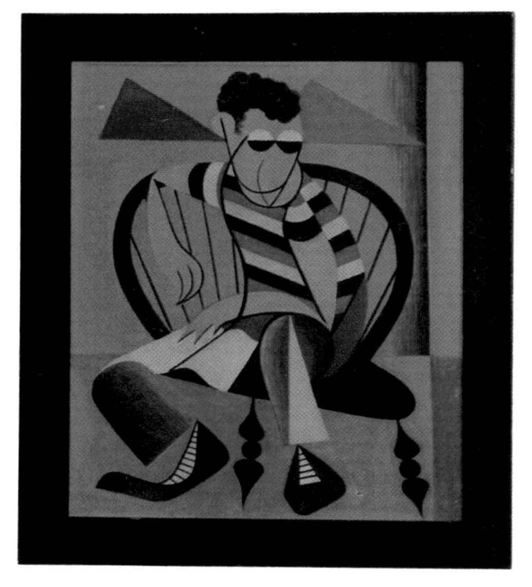

115

114

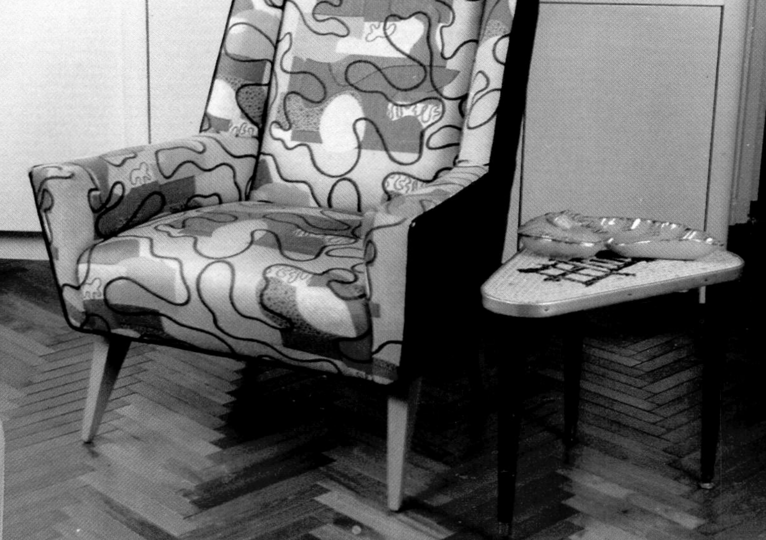

117

116

118

118 "World's Fair Treasure Island" pillow. Golden Gate International, 1939 World's Fair.

119

119 "Souvenir of Coney Island" pillow with green fringe. 17" square. Pre-1950s.

120 "Goodbye Prince Rupert." Atomic bomb fuses and other various subtleties surround him as he is whimsically flushing himself down the toilet.

120

121

122

121 A pink settee with toy poodles looking right at home sitting across it. Towering behind is a Moss Lighting Co. glitter lamp. Moss lamps are Lucite. This is white and clear in the shape of a street lamp.

122 This turquoise vinyl atomic lounge chair which reclines has a Coney Island souvenir pillow resting on it. The 1950s seahorse above was an advertising display for a diner in Texas in the fifties. The clock is by Howard Miller.

123

123 A 1950s bedroom. The ameoba shaped coffee table to the left holds a Moss lamp, comedy and tragedy, with spinners and a music box. To the right of the bed is a mosaic coffee table with the same Moss lamp. The wall displays a mosaic representing Easter Island. The bed has a 1950s fabric bedspread similar to a Calder mobile pattern.

124 Jensen tile wall hangings of French-looking characters hang above a Carmen Miranda doll who was extremely popular at the time. The chair is covered in a fabulous 1950s atomic fabric next to a 1950s flowerpot.

125 Atomic print chair has a black and pink Moss lamp behind it which spins. Also, notice the black poodle napkin holder which holds 1950s greeting cards.

124

125

126 Abstract design textile, almost cartoon-like.

127 Black with orange and white figural motif.

128 Incredibly heavily woven tapestry with tiny drawings.

TEXTILES

Abstract, Atomic, Representational and Floral

Textiles are probably the most prominent example of 1950s popular culture, because the textiles are manifest in their sense of whimsy, with brilliant and vibrant patterns. Many of the textiles are blends of rayon with silk, and some are cotton. The bark cloth was a heavier, textured cloth that was less expensive but available in the same wonderful designs.

In textiles, perhaps more than in any other material, the influence of fine art was displayed. Alexander Calder's modern shapes and colors in mobiles created a sense of humor that was brought to textile design. Calder's use of bright primary colors made his mobiles very engaging and their abstract shapes hinted at a futuristic style so popular during the time. The balance and movement of the shapes created a feeling of well being and optimism. Similarly, the works of Jean Arp and Joan Miro are salient in these textile designs.

In 1947, Jackson Pollack made his first large-scale action painting of abstract expressionism which was imitated in textiles and in fashion. Such great designers as Lucienne Day transformed the works of fine arts into designs and patterns for the applied arts. She had a talent for taking an art design and making it work in textile design.

The 1950s textiles were influenced by factors other than fine arts as well. For instance, architecture and furniture's curvilinear shapes and themes attracted abstract designs on the fabrics. An amoeboid-shaped couch deserved a wonderful abstract print to be displayed on it.

Interestingly, the new, modernistic and abstract designs were brought to America through a Scandinavian influence. Knoll International, a Scandinavian firm, introduced its fabrics to the United States in the early 1940s. In the fifties, America saw the Americanization of the German Bauhaus designs. Affiliates such as Charles Eames, Eero Saarinen, and Florence Knoll were producing wondrous new furniture based on completely new forms. The textiles of the period followed their lead, so although designer furniture by Herman Miller or Knoll International was highly priced, the textiles that derived from the aesthetics were not. These fabrics fell into the essence of the 1950s by being available to many more people.

Whimsical patterns also provided an antidote to the drabness and austerity of the war years. With the luxuries that abounded in the United States, whimsy was the symbol of frivolity. Stylized icons of everyday life in the household were also ubiquitous as fabrics actually displayed television sets, cars, flying saucers, and molecules, to name a few.

Famous traditional floral designs on textiles were always present, but the abstracts and representational fabrics represented a new, post-war attitude. Anything which represented the modern was embraced in admiration. Amoeba shapes, images of atoms, and Western scenes, they were all icons of popular American culture.

In the following decades, these same fabrics, with familiar ameoboid, abstract and molecular designs, fell into the terminology of "kitsch." They were so often imitated and available to everyone, like so many other objects imitated in the fifties, that they were no longer seen for their unique quality. Eventually, in the 1990s, these same designs are popular once again among collectors who revel in their brilliant colors and magnificent designs. Many now realize their quality, and the fifties textiles grow in collectibility.

126

127

128

129 **131** **133**

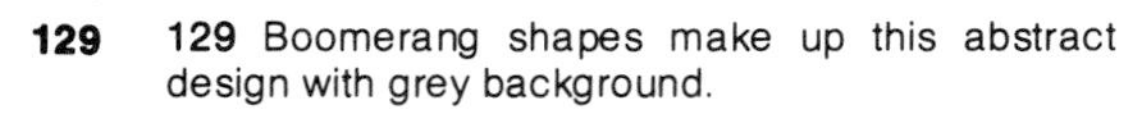

129 Boomerang shapes make up this abstract design with grey background.

131 Abstract fabric with grey/green background. No pattern name.

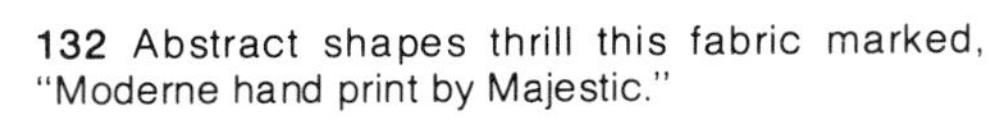

132 Abstract shapes thrill this fabric marked, "Moderne hand print by Majestic."

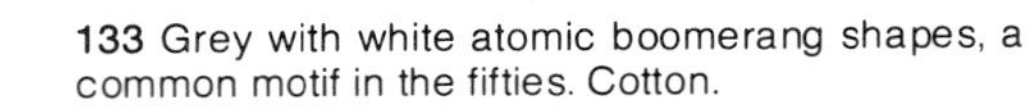

133 Grey with white atomic boomerang shapes, a common motif in the fifties. Cotton.

130 Curtain with science and futuristic motif.

130 **132**

134

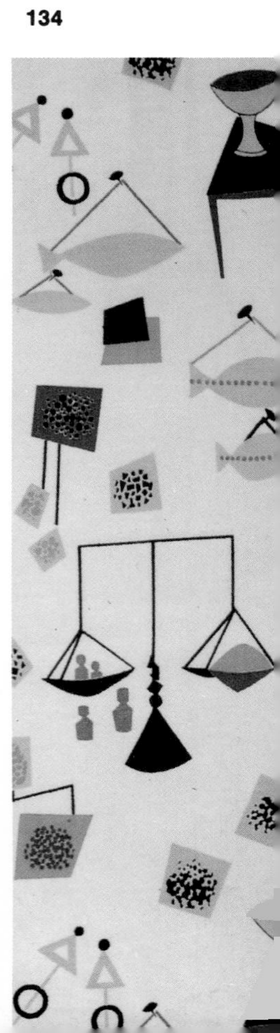

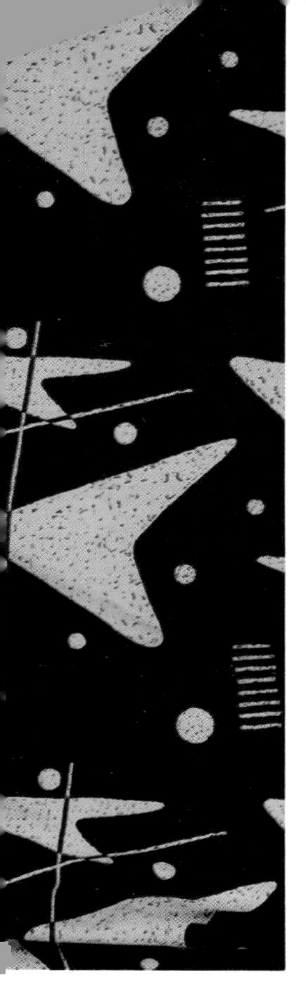

135

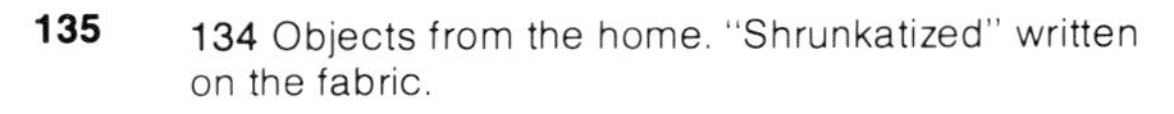

134 Objects from the home. "Shrunkatized" written on the fabric.

135 Textile with grey background and abstract peacock feathers.

136 Another Calder-like mobile design displayed on a fabric.

136

137

137 Abstract shapes make up an exquisite pattern on a blue/green background.

138 Olive green fabric marked, "Cofabco Vat print fully guaranteed." The abstract geometric shapes remind one of an Alexander Calder pattern. Resembles fifties lighting accessories.

138

139

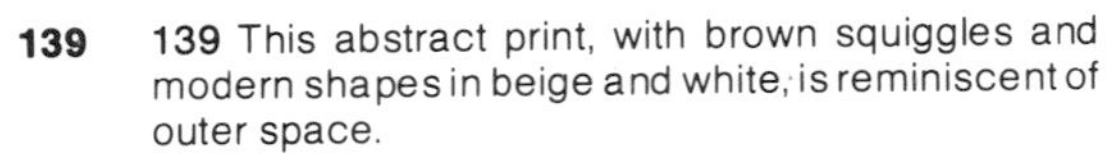

139 This abstract print, with brown squiggles and modern shapes in beige and white, is reminiscent of outer space.

140 Sample fabric with a grey background and abstract figures that look like birds. The ubiquitous fifties colors of pink, black and grey are used.

140

141

141 Blue squiggle, cotton canvas, with atomic motif.

142 Atomic pattern, grey fabric with atomic shapes. No label.

143 Abstract squiggled design with various colors. Notice the Miro, Matisse, and Chagall influence.

142

143

144

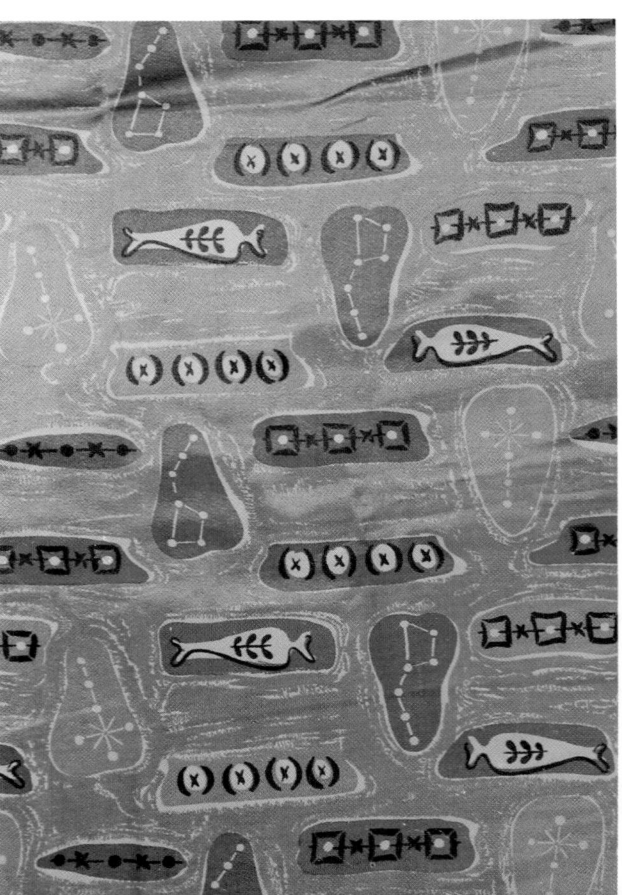

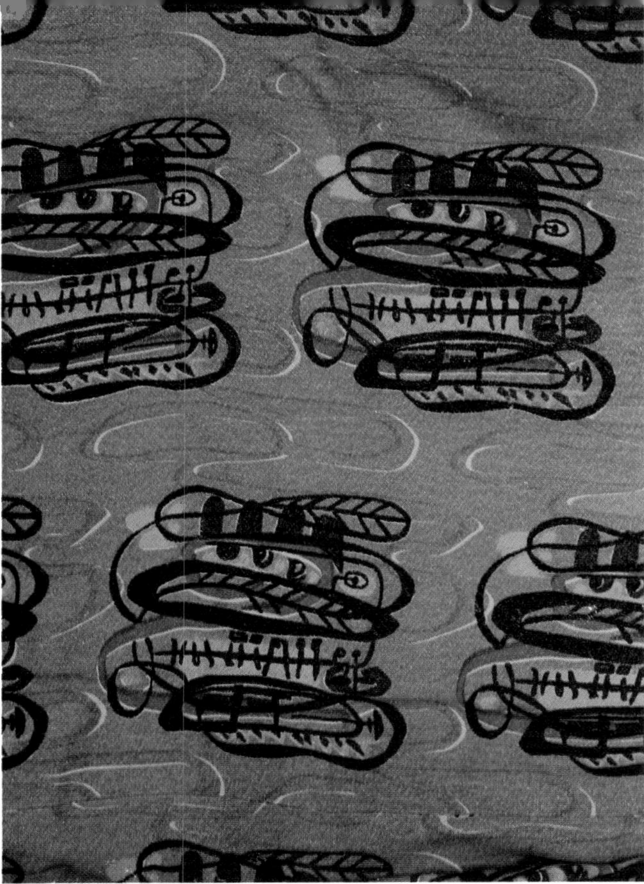

145

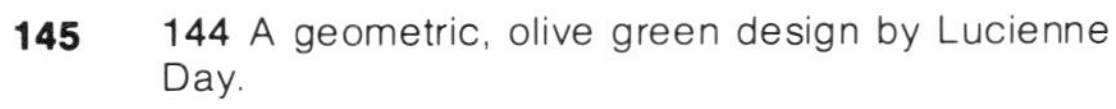

144 A geometric, olive green design by Lucienne Day.

145 Green background hand print abstract pattern called Fleura. Designed by Ruth Reeves.

146 An abstract geometric print with harlequin motif. The label on this fabric reads, "Reflect Hand print."

146

147

147 Pink and black atomic print as if electrons were shooting across the fabric.

148 Another very abstract design on this fabric with light blue squiggles.

148

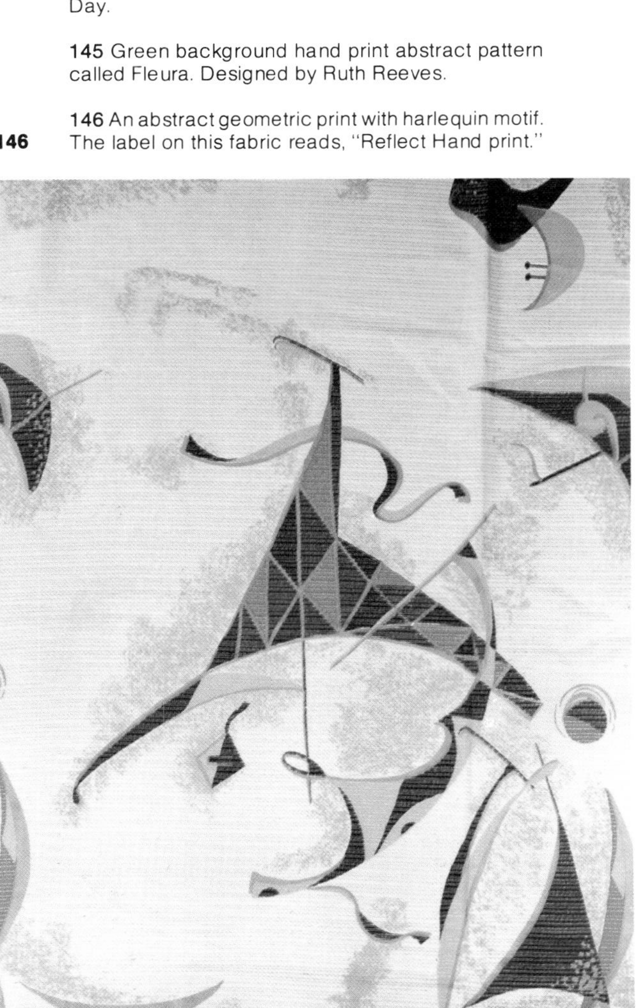

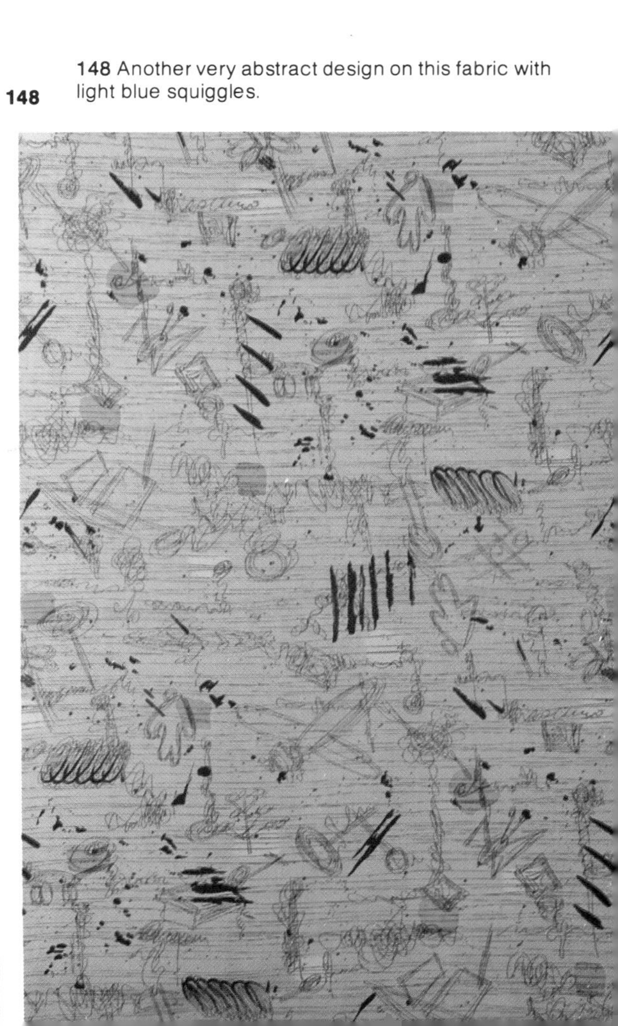

149 Golfing scene titled, "Under 80" by the S.M Hexter Co." Late 1940s.

150 Wonderful wilderness scene with tropical trees and black panthers.

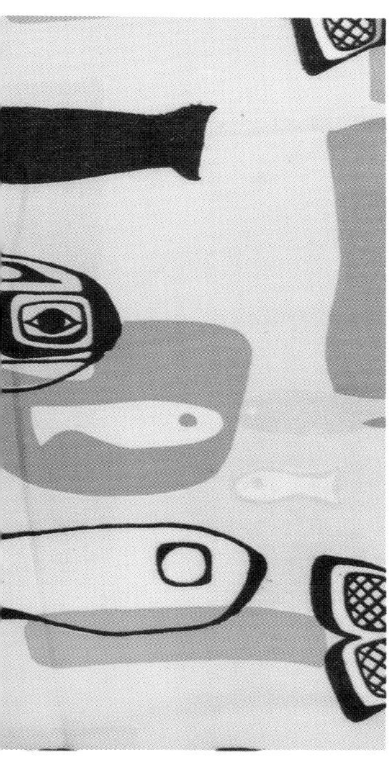

151 "Crackled jugs" in purples and grey give a wonderful effect.

152 An abstract view of the New York skyline. You can see the Statue of Liberty and the Brooklyn Bridge.

153 Fun fish pattern on a bolt of fabric marked "Puritan Vat Print."

154 Abstract fish motif with pale colors and abstract shapes. Goodall Fabrics, Inc. New York. Cotton, rayon & mohair.

155 Dark brown textile with wonderful abstract design by Lucienne Day.

156 "Hand Print Ballet" Representational and abstract. Very much like an artist's painting.

157 Moulin Rouge print with the Toulouse Lautrec posters.

157

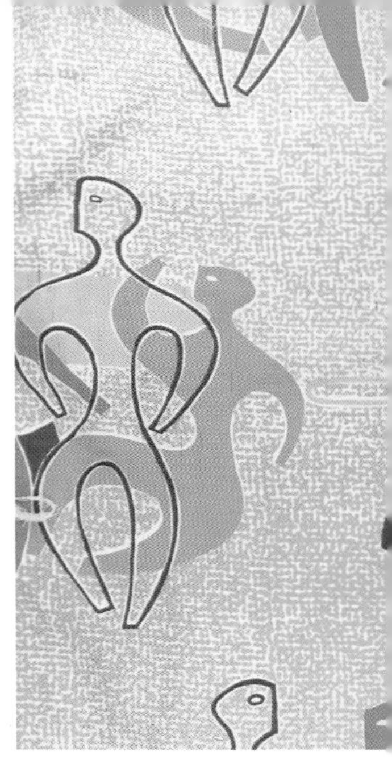

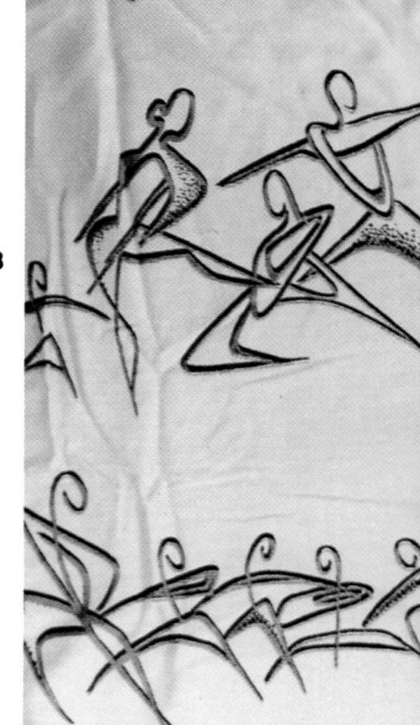

158

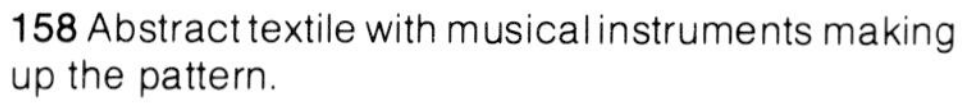

158 Abstract textile with musical instruments making up the pattern.

159 Another "Hand Print Ballet" pattern, this one lighthearted, less crowded, and more "subtle" in pink.

160 Abstracted dancers with tan and blue rugged lines.

161 Abstracted dancers, white with gold and black figures. A figural or representational fabric.

162 Abstract textile design in black and green, with wild geometrics suggesting human figures.

163 Very abstract pattern on this black and white textile from the fifties.

164 Fabric for children of clown faces on a gold background. A signature fabric with an unreadable signature.

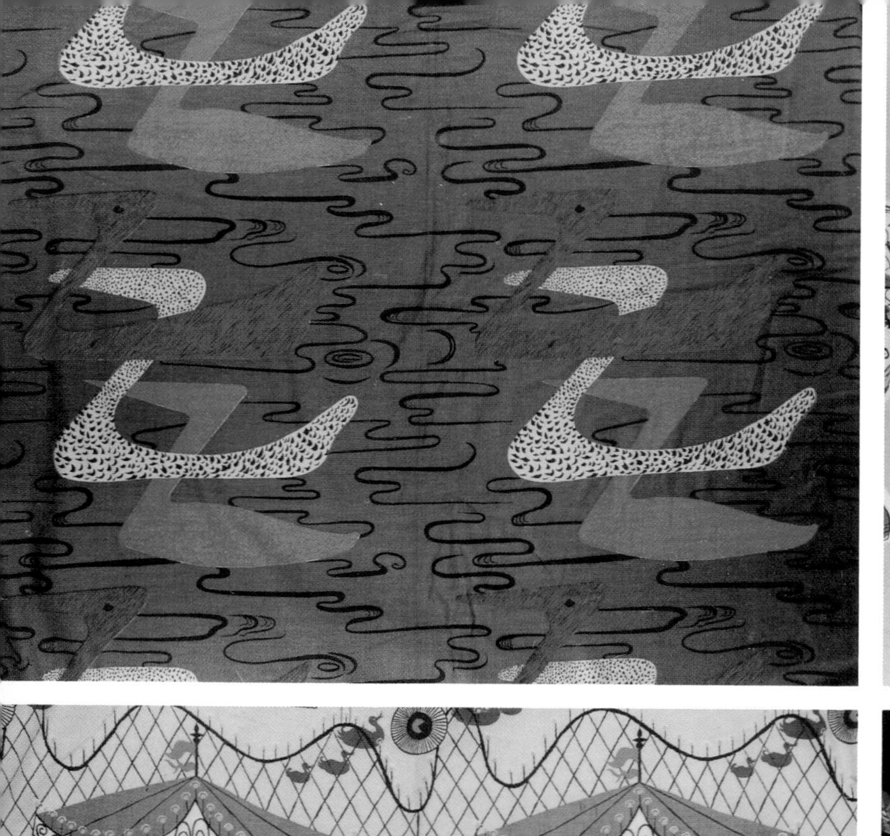

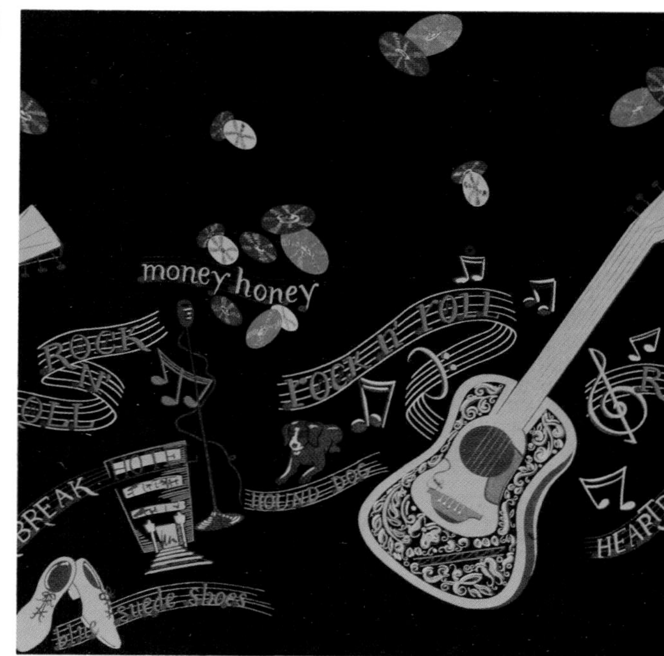
money honey
ROCK N ROLL
HOUND DOG

166

171

172

168

165 Dark green squiggles with abstract ducks.

166 Fabric with men and women in various scenes on a light blue background.

167 Fabric with a carousel pattern. No label.

168 Black fabric with cool rock and roll motifs floating across the bottom.

169 White background with abstract design giving the appearance of the sails of ships. Marked, "Saison Happily Married Fabrics."

170 Figural textile with girls and boys grooving in various tasks common in the fifties.

171 By Fuller Fabrics. The pattern name is "Femme Ecoutant" by D.B. Fuller and Co. Brown, white and black.

172 Rock and roll print in cotton on a pale green background with tiny figures of girls and boys dancing to music.

173 "Happy Harry and his Rock and Roll Five," you can even see the music on this piece of fabric!

173

175

180

177

181

174 Green bark cloth with a Hawaiian floral motif.

175 Another floral fabric made of rayon with large pink roses.

176 Floral textile made of bark cloth with large floral motif, somewhat tropical.

177 Grey background with pink birds in a floral motif.

178 Grey background floral textile with pinapple motif made of bark cloth.

179 Radiant floral motif on a red background. A 1940s fabric with large grey flowers. Marked, "A Sprectrum Original Vat Color."

180 Rayon textile with gold, red and blue birds of paradise throughout.

181 Delicate hand painted floral fabric with navy and purplish flowers.

182 A more conservative pattern than some of the others, a rayon, floral textile with white background. The flowers look as though they are painted on with all the colors.

179

182

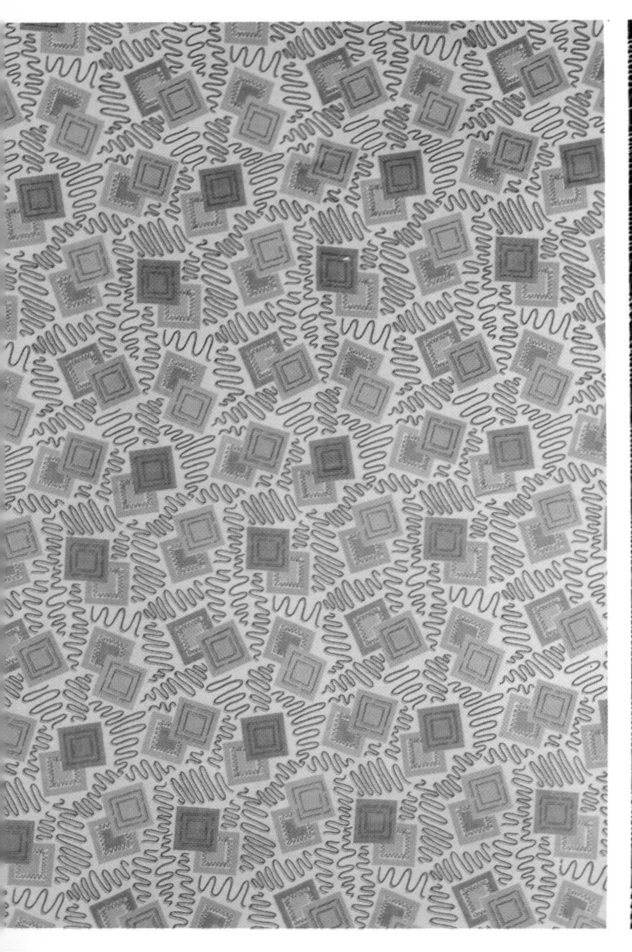

183

184

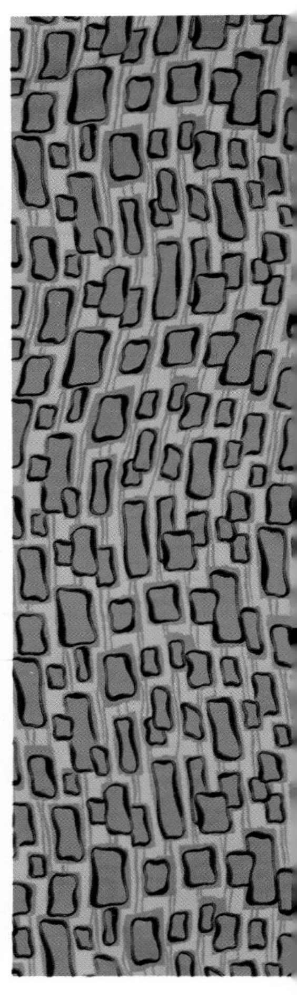

183 Fantastic squiggle pattern on cotton, grey and pink squares.

184 Rayon squiggle fabric, pink and green on dark blue.

185 Light blue geometric textile made of rayon, on a white background.

186 Navy background with red and white chips floating throughout.

187 Rayon, abstract design textile with red, pink, yellow and white on a greyish background.

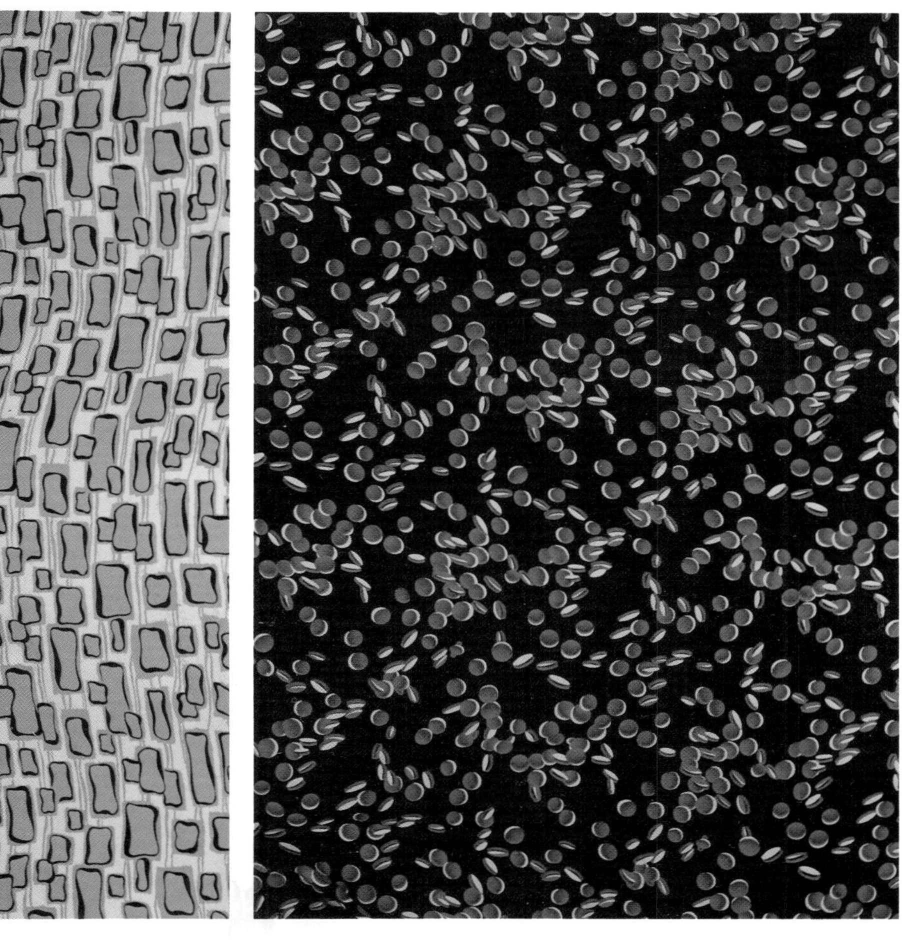

185

186

187

ART FROM THE CLOSET

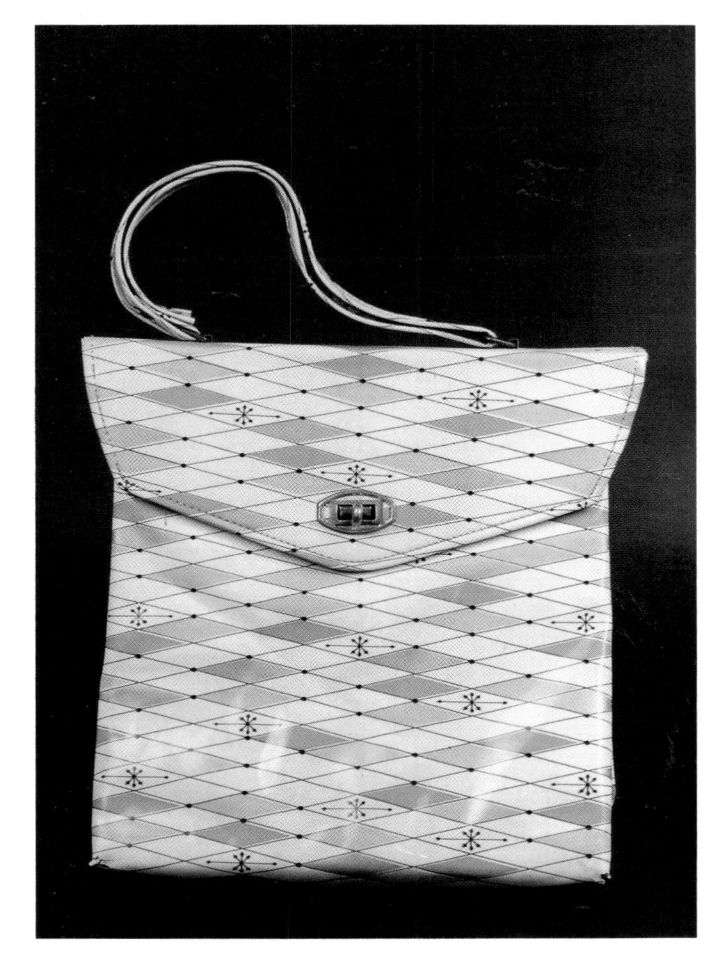

189

188

LUCITE & VINYL HANDBAGS

Ladies' handbags of the 1950s were incredible, literally. They were so out of this world, that they are extremely collectible today, in the 1990s, for their artistic and whimsical qualities.

The boxy-shaped bag was in style, and the hard, new plastic materials, Lucite and vinyl, fit this mold perfectly. Women who wanted the modern look found it in the new materials which were becoming everpresent in consumer products. Handbag manufacturers such as Llewellyn, Wilardy and Rialto siezed upon a market which thrived for a futuristic and unique look. They produced bags of plastic which could be tinted different colors for elegant effects. A new craze was soon in full force.

The popularity of these bags lasted about ten years, from the late forties to the late fifties. Almost everyone owned one, from the young teeny-bopper with a pink bag with gold glitter throughout, to the sophisticated lady carrying a clear bag with rhinestones. The 1950s introduced the idea that each outfit required a new handbag to match, and manufacturers were more then welcome to meet the demand.

Soon, the market became competitive as manufacturers tried to outdue one another by adding the frivolities and wild decorations to their bags that make them so collectible today. Shapes were created to look like anything from pagodas to birdcages and guitars! Glitter was added, and metal filigree trims, even fake flowers to give the appearance of a coffin. As the bags became more and more specialized, they actually began to decline in popularity. The average woman soon found the bags too frivolous for everyday use.

188 Vinyl handbag showing La Boutique, a ladies hat and dress shop. Label reads, "Sara's Las Vegas Nevada."

189 Wonderful harlequin vinyl bag with the all-over diamond pattern.

The craze for plastic handbags also diminished when cheaper copies were made. A thirty- to fifty-dollar bag could be copied by a competitor with a flimsier plastic at a much lower price. Women also found the boxy shapes to be cumbersome and too fixed in shape to hold all their essentials. The softer vinyl bags were good alternatives to this boxy style, and the modern look was temporarily maintained with this more pliable material.

The vinyl bags actually, were extraordinarily ironic. Often these bags were made of straw with a vinyl covering, or were made entirely of vinyl. Displaying various scenes common for the decade, they reached the hearts of many. Women would carry underwater scenes

190

191

190 Straw vinyl bag with two cats. Label reads, "Princess Charming by Atlas, Hollywood, Florida."

191 Bird and cat bag by "Josef's of the Village."

192 Galloping horse vinyl bag.

192

with them to go shopping, frontices of boutiques, pirates, mermaids, animals, even confetti to connote a spirit of frivolity.

Finally, in the late 1950s, the plastic bags all began to look a little too impractical. As Europe regained its strength as the fashion capital of the world, the American sensation of the plastic handbag seemed to dwindle. Women soon were choosing a beaded or leather European bag over their sleek black plastic evening bag. The vinyl and plastic bags were being stored in the attic not to be rediscovered again until the late 1980s. Today, these whimsical, artistic and elaborate bags bring equivalent prices to match their outrageous designs.

193

194

195

193 A red heron graces this handbag.

194 Mermaid under water scene. No label.

195 Grey felt sailfish bag. Label reads, "Souré Bag New York."

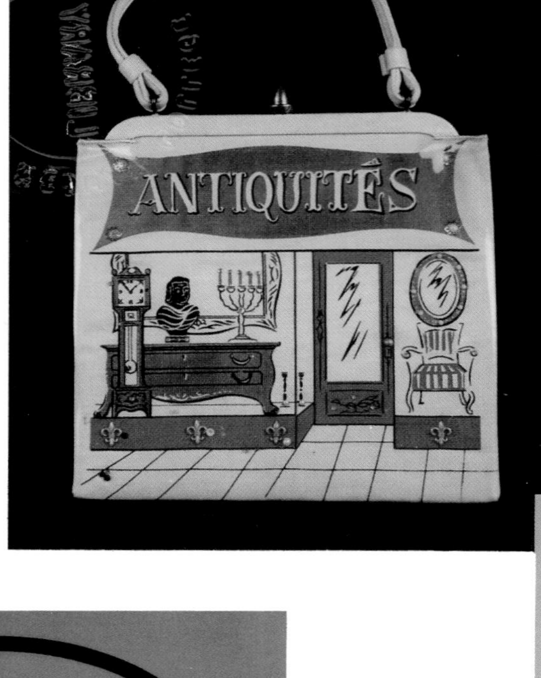

196

197

198

199

200

196 Vinyl bag displaying an antiques shop, "Antiquités." Label reads, "Souré."

197 Whimsical cocktail hour box-style bag. Label reads, "Kustam by Kitty."

198 Vinyl bag with an atomic fifties print. No label.

199 Black leather bag with gold record that says, "Paris, New York, Rome." Label reads, "Prestige Bag."

200 Pirate's cove bag made of straw and vinyl. Very picturesque, even looks hand made. No label.

202

201

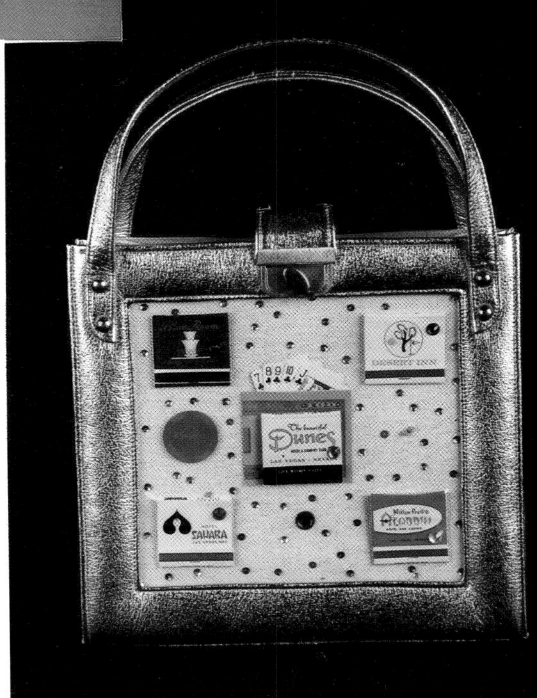

204

203

205

201 Great vinyl bag with a harlequin and dancer.

202 Hat stand for the hallway with hats on it, vinyl. No label.

203 Vinyl bag with theatre tickets interposed. Various theatres are shown on the tickets, for example, the Imperial theatre dated June 7. No label.

204 Vinyl bag with Las Vegas matchbooks. Label reads, "Faye Mell Design. Mfg. Fleurette Inc. Miami Florida."

205 Grey and red felt telephone bag with the word, "Hello". No label.

206

207

208

209

206 Harlequin bag with a Picasso-like feel. No label.

207 Black velvet choo choo train bag. No label.

208 A rhinestone sun and raindrops glisten on this vinyl bag. Label reads, "Bag by Llewellyn."

209 Fabulous vinyl fish bag. No label.

210

210 Long, black felt squiggle clutch. No label.

211 Marvelous vinyl, black and gold squiggle handbag with glitter handle. No label.

212 Vinyl squiggle bag with black and grey. Label reads, "Micha of Coronet."

213 Vinyl fish makeup bag. No label.

211

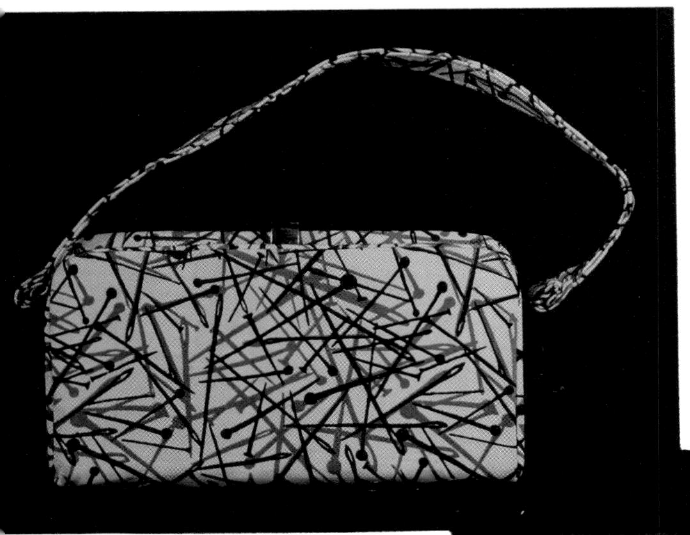

212

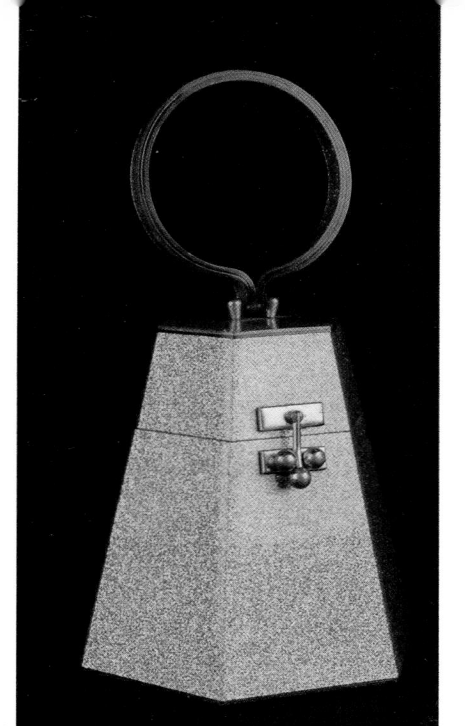

214

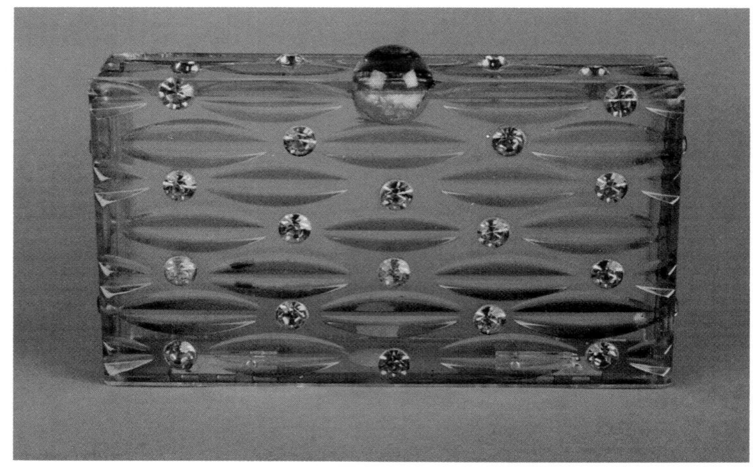

215

216

217

218

214 A very rare, plastic glitter bag with a hexagonal shape. Maker unknown.

215 Amber tinted plastic bag with large rhinestones, no label.

216 Patricia of Miami black and gold squiggle bag. Long and narrow shape with a clear lid.

217 Elegant black plastic clutch bag with rhinestone fastener. A Wilardy Original.

218 Kidney-shaped gold glitter bag made of Lucite. No label.

219 Black plastic shell bag with a red lining inside. A Lewsid Jewel by Llewellyn.

219

220

221

222

223

220 This bag of semi-transparent lucite, with threads of black and silver, is finished with a metal trim.

221 Multi-colored glitter guitar-shaped plastic bag. Unreadable label.

222 Black Lucite bag with abstract white lines throughout. No label.

223 Gold confetti bag with black trim, oval shaped, no label.

225

224

224 A very interesting bee bag. By Nettie Rosenstein. Black satin.

225 Plastic black and gold, square glitter confetti bag.

226 Confetti-filled bags. Multi-colored rounded confetti clutch with clear handle; multi-colored squared-off clutch; multi-colored compact case with chain; and multi-colored clutch, marked "Shoreham. Shell-lite."

227 Lucite bag with gold pineapples on lid. No label.

228 Multi-colored glitter bag with clear handle, marked "David's 5th Ave."

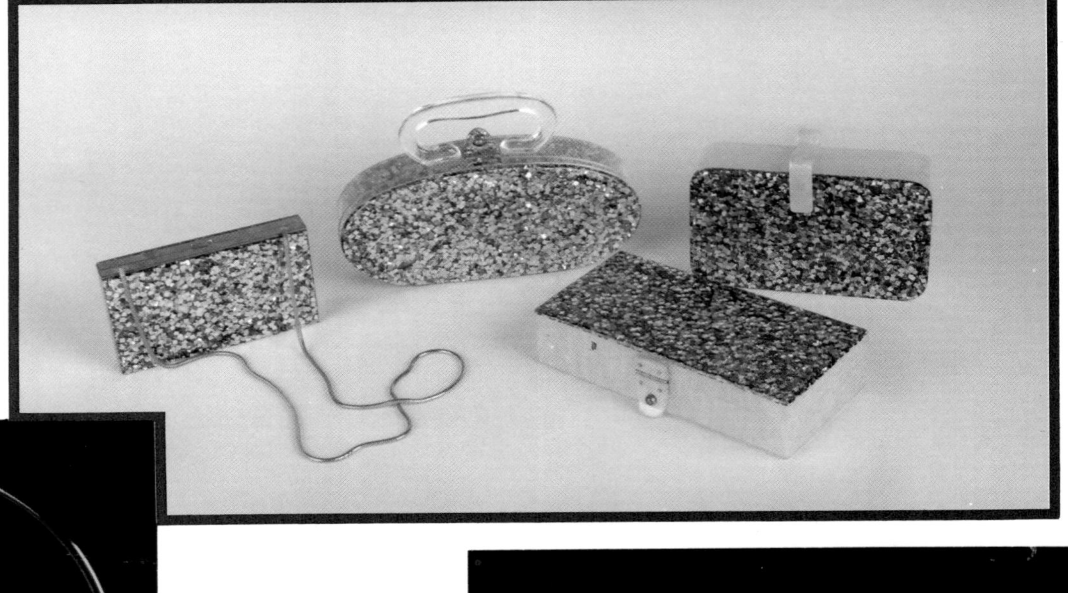

227

228

229

230

231

232

233

234

229 Clear lucite and rhinestone bag. "Maxims." 9.5" x 7.25".

230 Black bag with green rhinestones in lines.

231 Multi-colored glitter clutch made by Rialto, New York.

232 Musical compact in its case.

233 Black bag with large rhinestones; small bag covered with rhinestones, black and glitter striped clutch; and a black bag with lines of rhinestones. Makers unknown.

234 Studded bag in the shape of a trunk. Vinyl with metal studs. Early Judith Leiber, c. 1960s.

235

FASHION ACCESSORIES

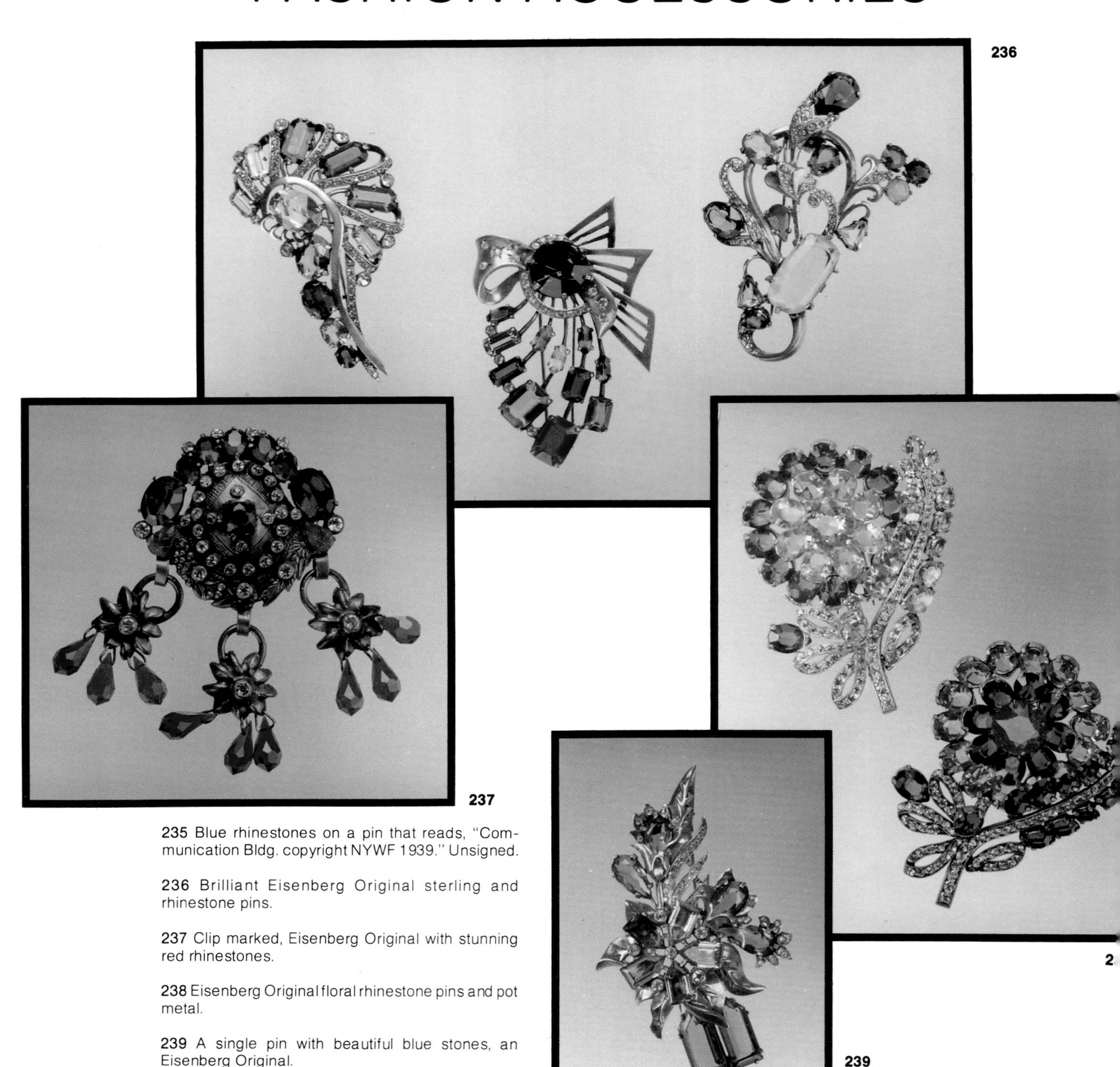

236

237

239

2

235 Blue rhinestones on a pin that reads, "Communication Bldg. copyright NYWF 1939." Unsigned.

236 Brilliant Eisenberg Original sterling and rhinestone pins.

237 Clip marked, Eisenberg Original with stunning red rhinestones.

238 Eisenberg Original floral rhinestone pins and pot metal.

239 A single pin with beautiful blue stones, an Eisenberg Original.

240

1

240 The Mexican influence is evident in these pieces. The floral piece is signed, Eisenberg Original. The others are unsigned, but attributed to Eisenberg Original.

241 Three figural Eisenberg Original pins from the forties.

242 Three (imitation turquoise etc.) Eisenberg Originals pins influenced by Mexico with a Sante Fe look.

242

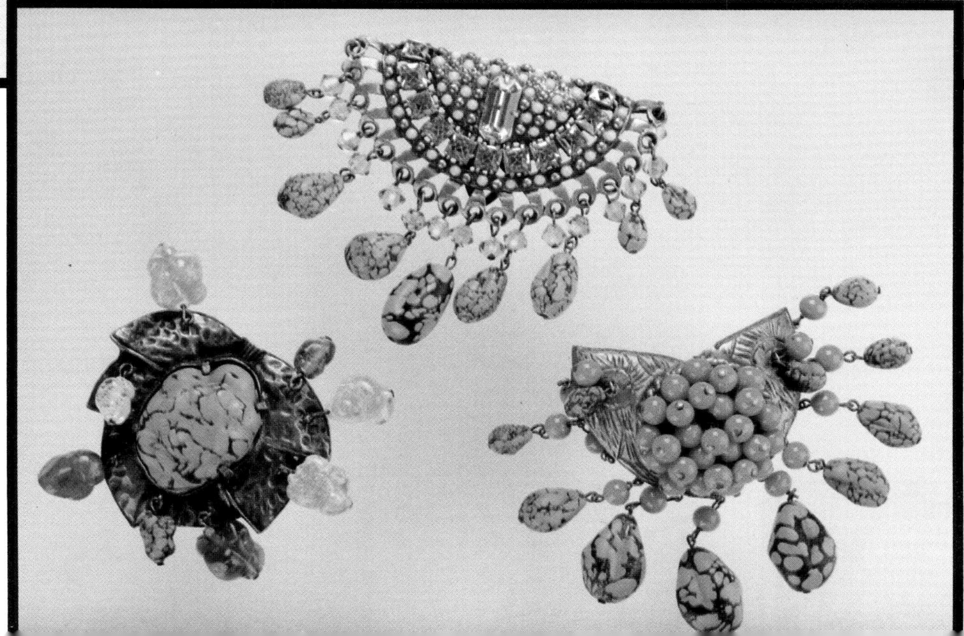

243

24

245 Three larger bracelets by Hobé with multi colored crystals and filigree.

246 Two large Hobé brooches, the oval is 4.5" an the round is 3.5".

243 Two beautifully jeweled compacts by Hobé and a box by Hobé.

244 Three brooches by Hobé, with beautifully colored rhinestones and filigree.

245

246

247

249

48

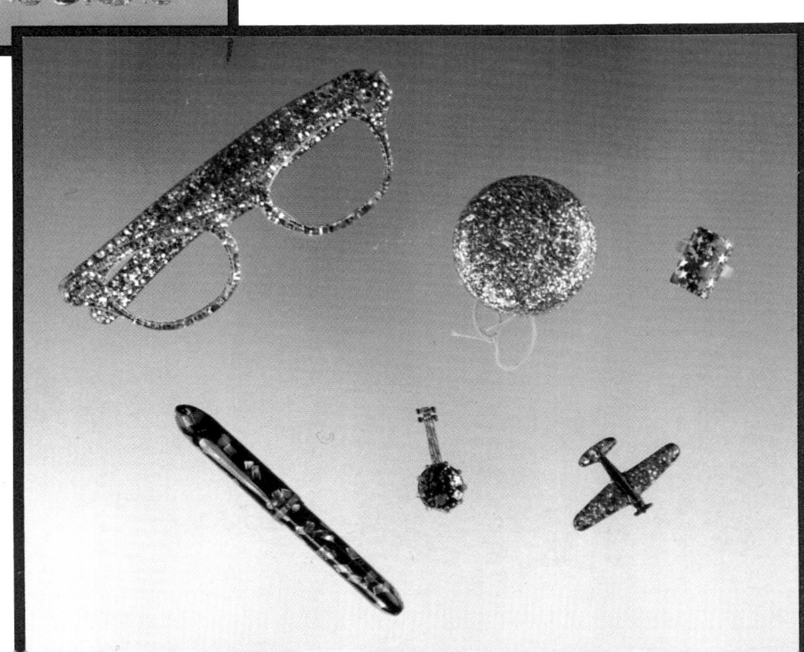

250

247 Necklace and bracelets by Hobé with silver bells and crystals, this gives an Indian look to the jewelry.

248 Unsigned bracelet with rhinestones and enamel leaves.

249 A Charles Armour turtle pin. His jewelry is very rare. He designed clothing at the same time as Nettie Rosenstein, late 1930s-early 40s.

250 Assorted glitter items: sunglasses, yoyo, ring, pen, and two figural pins in the shapes of a ukelele and an airplane.

251 Various glitter or confetti plastic bracelets, some with stars, some with lines, and some with squares.

252 Fabulous glitter compacts.

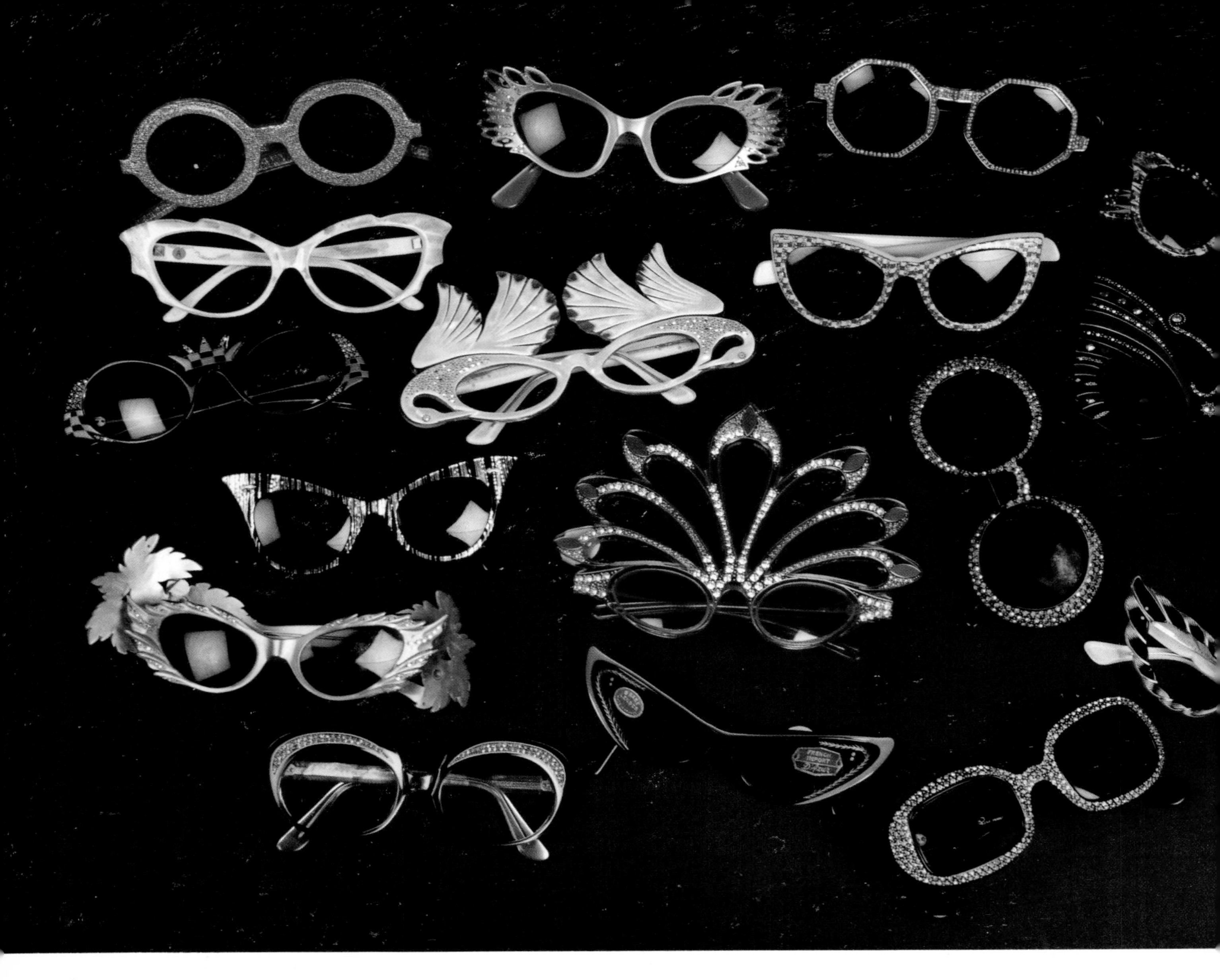

253

25

253 Various sunglasses from the forties and fifties.

254 Display glitter glasses. 5.5″ h. x 17″ w.

255 Various and funky glitter earrings.

256 Eyeglass cases with various fifties designs and themes.

255

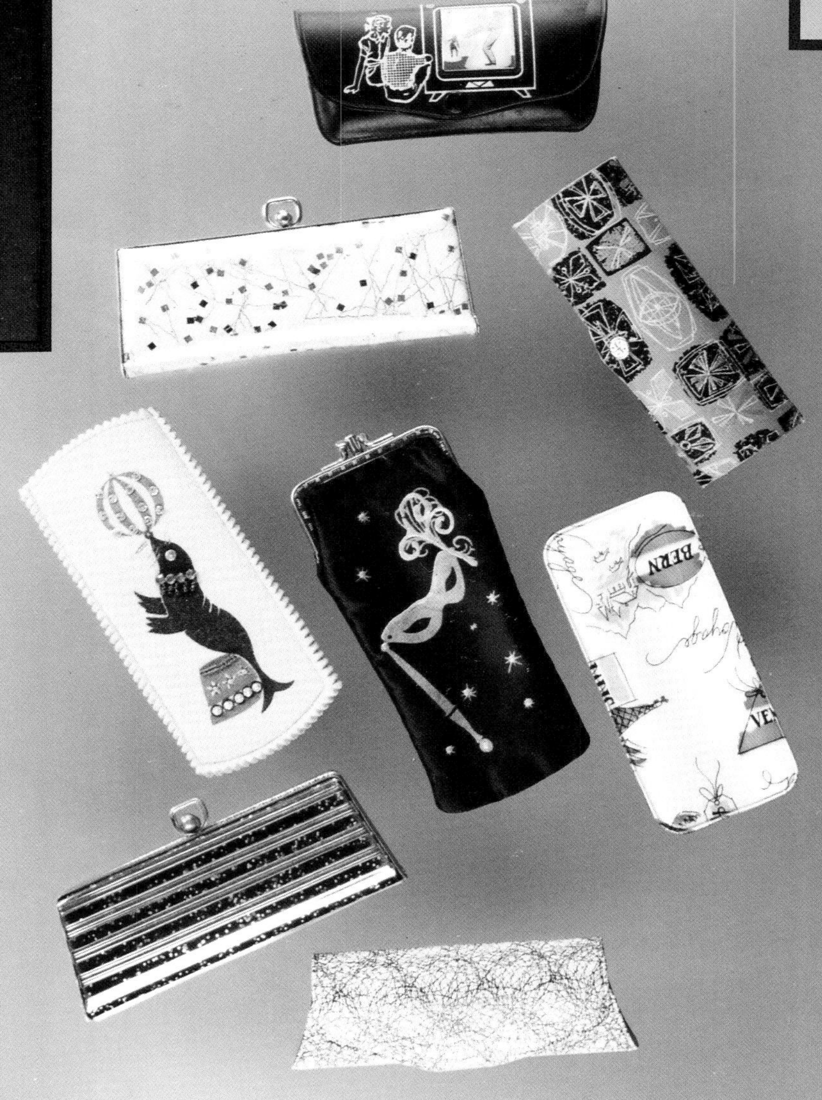

256

257

DANIELS & FISHER

258

byron
FIFTH AVENUE
NEW YORK
ork
byron
fifth avenue
byron
FIFTH AVENUE
NEW YORK

259

260

261

257 Hatboxes with various themes from the fifties.

258 Daniels & Fisher hatbox.

259 Byron, Fifth Avenue New York hatbox.

260 A trio of Fifties hatboxes.

261 Four illustrated hatboxes.

262 Adam Hats hatboxes.

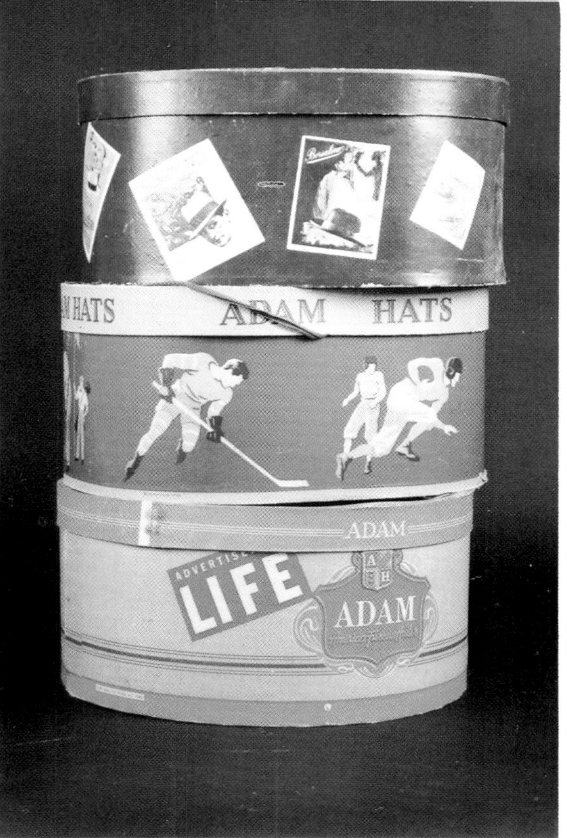

262

263

263 Rectangular, glittered 1939 World's Fair funky compacts. The round compacts in the center show various women and one with roses, all with glitter background.

264 Compact with baton twirlers.

265 Touristy Florida compact.

265

264

266

266 Cancan dancer on a deck of cards.

267 Playing cards with familiar fifties themes; space scene, conceptual cocktail containers, and harlequin masks.

268 Compacts that tie in with a lot of different themes: World's Fair with envelope, stamp and postmark; atomic stars with beads in center; Hawaiian hula dancer; scenic with palm tree and setting sun; airplane with cities; simplicity patterns; Scarlett O'Hara; palm tree; woman with a beaded dress and fabric skirt; and a bathing beauty.

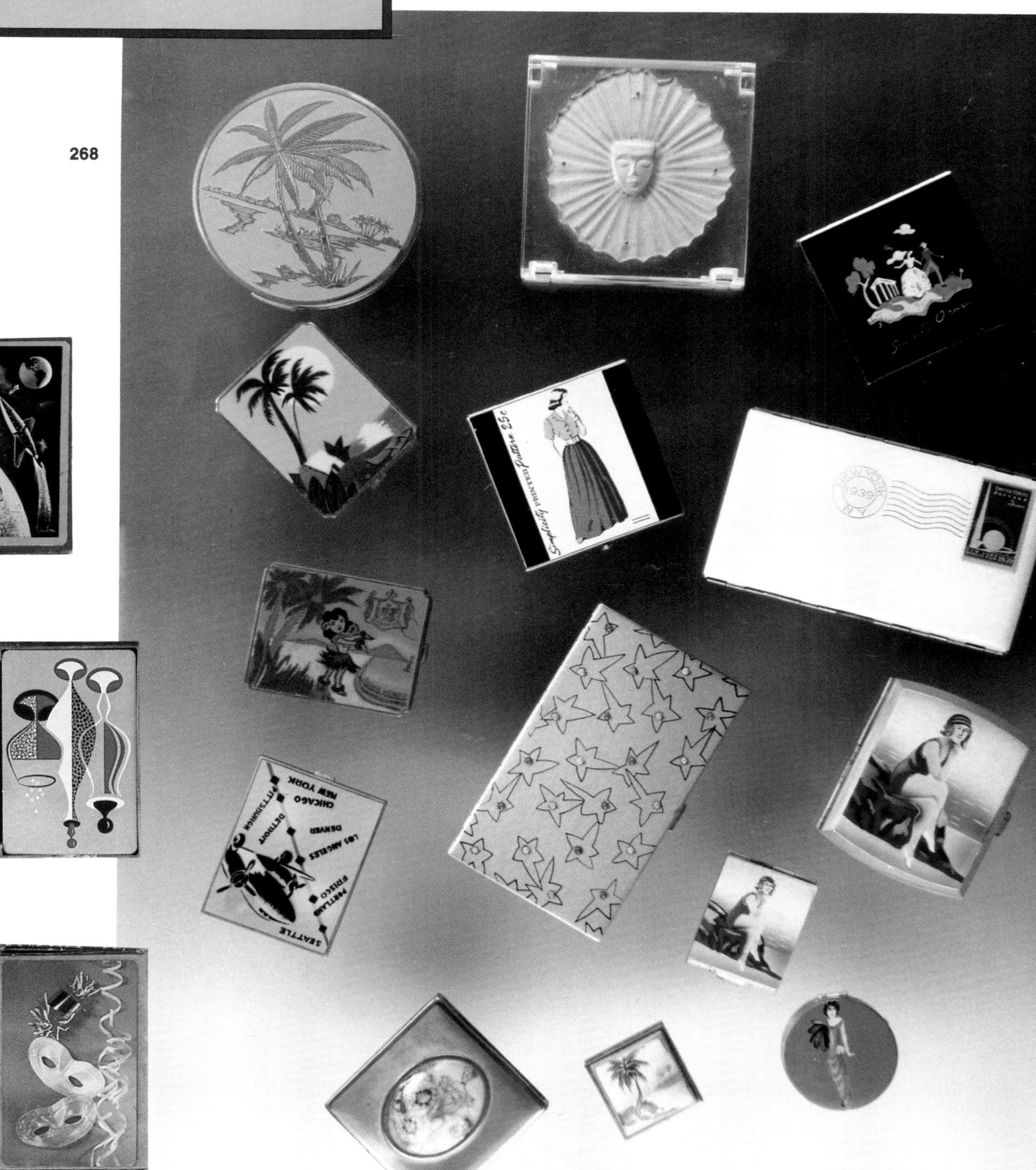

268

267

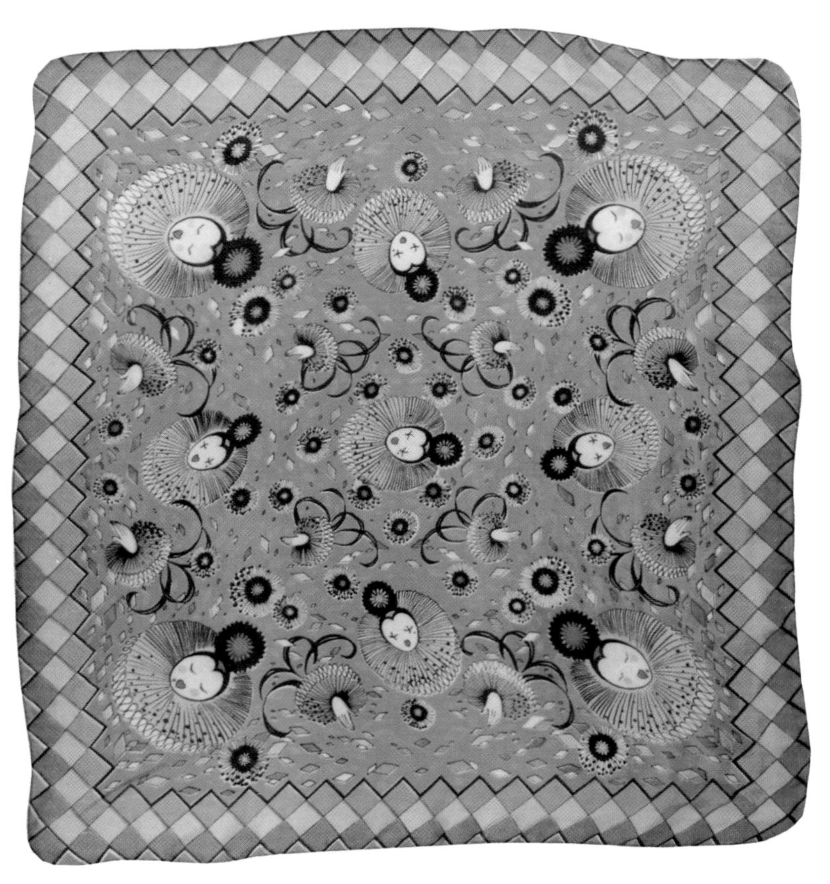

269

270

271

272

269 Harlequin scarf in a lively purple, pink and green. Powder puff ladies peer out among the other designs. Pure silk.

270 Brightly-colored, souvenir scarf, starring two dancers from tropical Catalina.

273

274

275

276

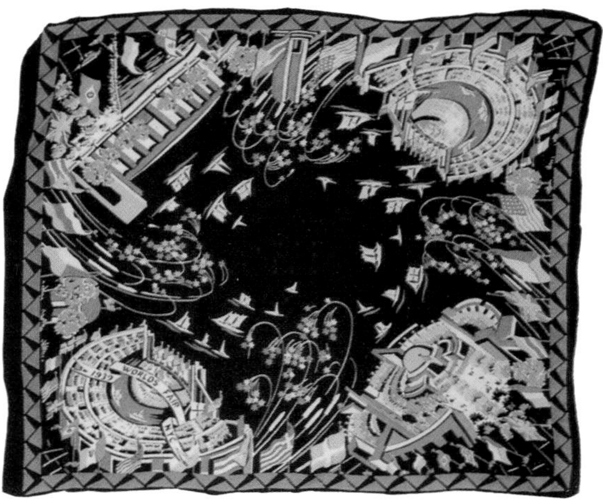

277

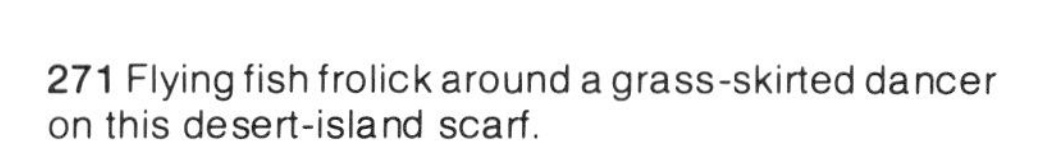

271 Flying fish frolick around a grass-skirted dancer on this desert-island scarf.

272 Silk circus scarf with poodles doing various tricks. No label.

273 Tiny pocket scarf of whimsical dancing couple signed, "John Held Jr."

274 1939 Pageant of the Pacific tablecloth.

275 Circus zebras and pink horses on striped backgrounds make a festive scarf.

276 Scarf of Sleeping Beauty, copyright, Walt Disney Productions.

277 Rayon scarf displaying the New York World's Fair, with orange around the border.

278

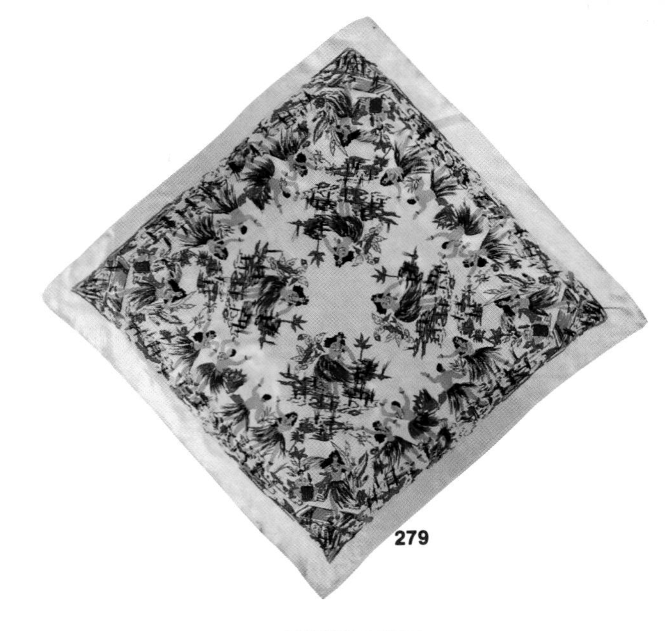

279

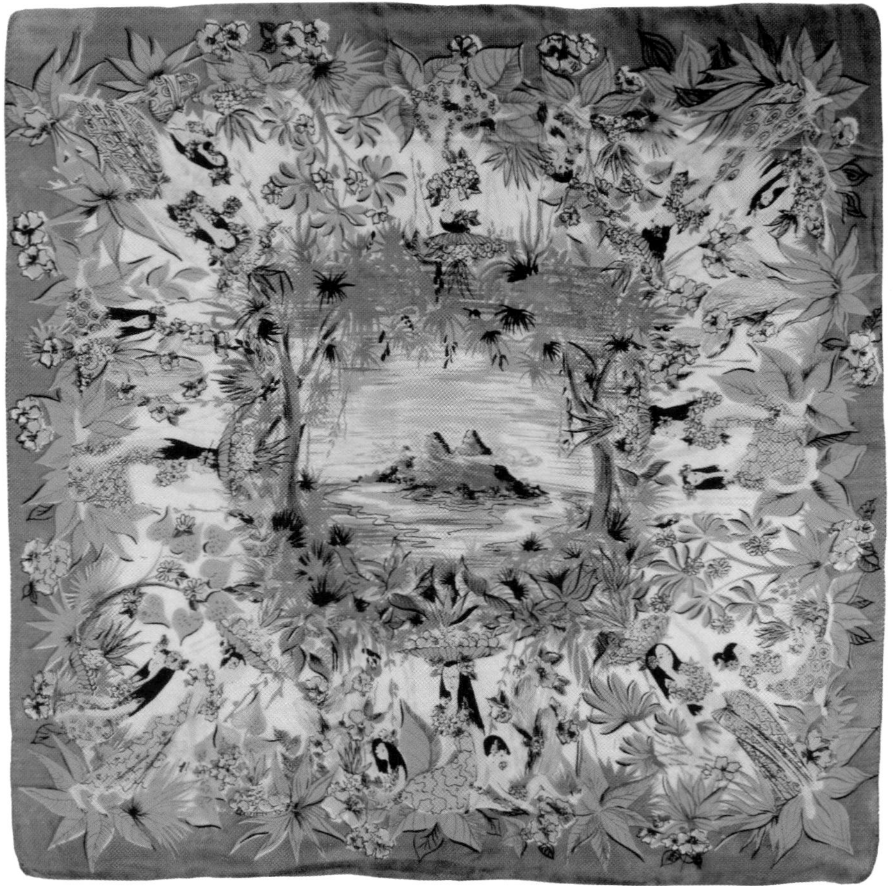

280

278 Silk scarf with another flamenco dancer motif.

279 Male and female dancers swish their grass skirts on this tropical scarf.

280 Hawaiian Luau scarf. White border with a volcano in middle. Silk.

281 Hawaiian rayon square with fringe with lai pattern.

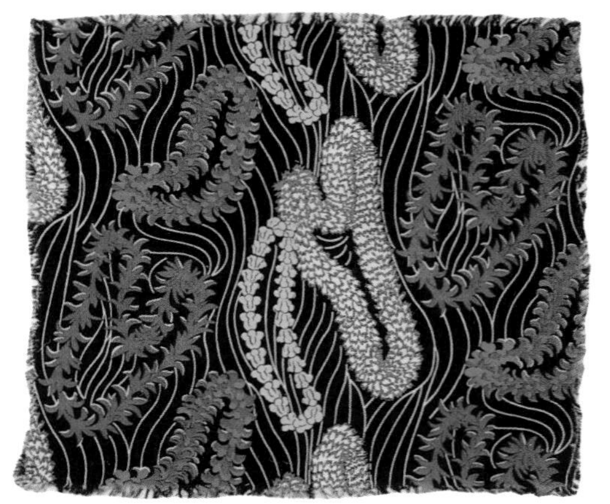

281

282 Native maidens peer through tropical foliage on this bright, black and fuschia scarf.

283 Silk scarf with a collage of luggage tags from ships, in fifties colors. No label.

284 Home Lines scarf advertising the Bahamas.

285 Flamingo scarf. Label reads, "Home Lines." Souvenir scarf from the ship company, cruise line, Home lines.

282

283

284

285

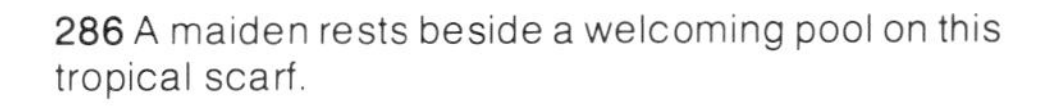

286 A maiden rests beside a welcoming pool on this tropical scarf.

287 A birdseye view of a charming cluster of islets, on a pale pastel scarf.

286

287

288

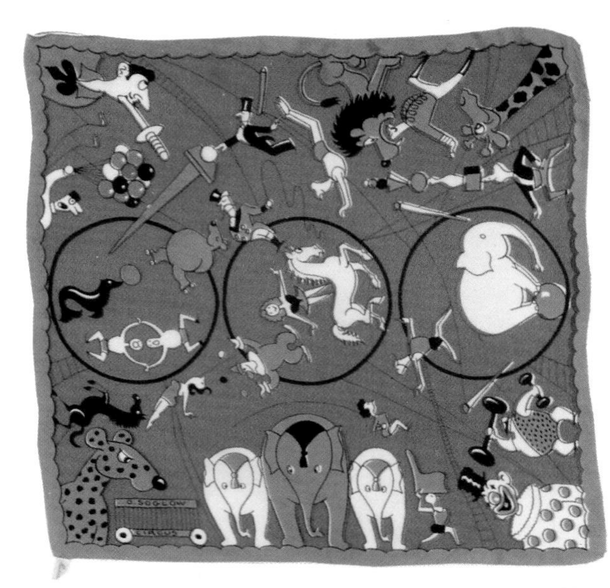

289

290

288 Stunning pure silk scarf with red and white zebras on a blue background.

289 Small square circus motif. "Richard A. Farrar."

290 Many of the great perfume bottles are listed on this scarf with green and navy border.

291 Another wonderful scarf illustrating a central park scene. Marked, "Glentex All Silk."

292 Silk pocket scarf of a small, California street cable car with a pink scarf flying in a pink cloud of dust. Signed "Tammi Keefe"

291

29

293

295

293 This scarf is interesting because not only is it reminiscent of a Degas painting, but it was also made in Occupied Japan. Marked, "Hand rolled, pure silk. A top hit fashion. Baar C. Beards Inc. Made in Occupied Japan."

294 Rayon scarf representing the New York World's Fair 1939. No label.

295 Rayon New York World's Fair scarf with chartreuse around the border.

296 A two-sided scarf, one shows another scene of buildings opening up to the pink sky. "Bon marché" is written on it.

297 Silk scarf with women holding assorted colored umbrellas. No label.

94

297

296

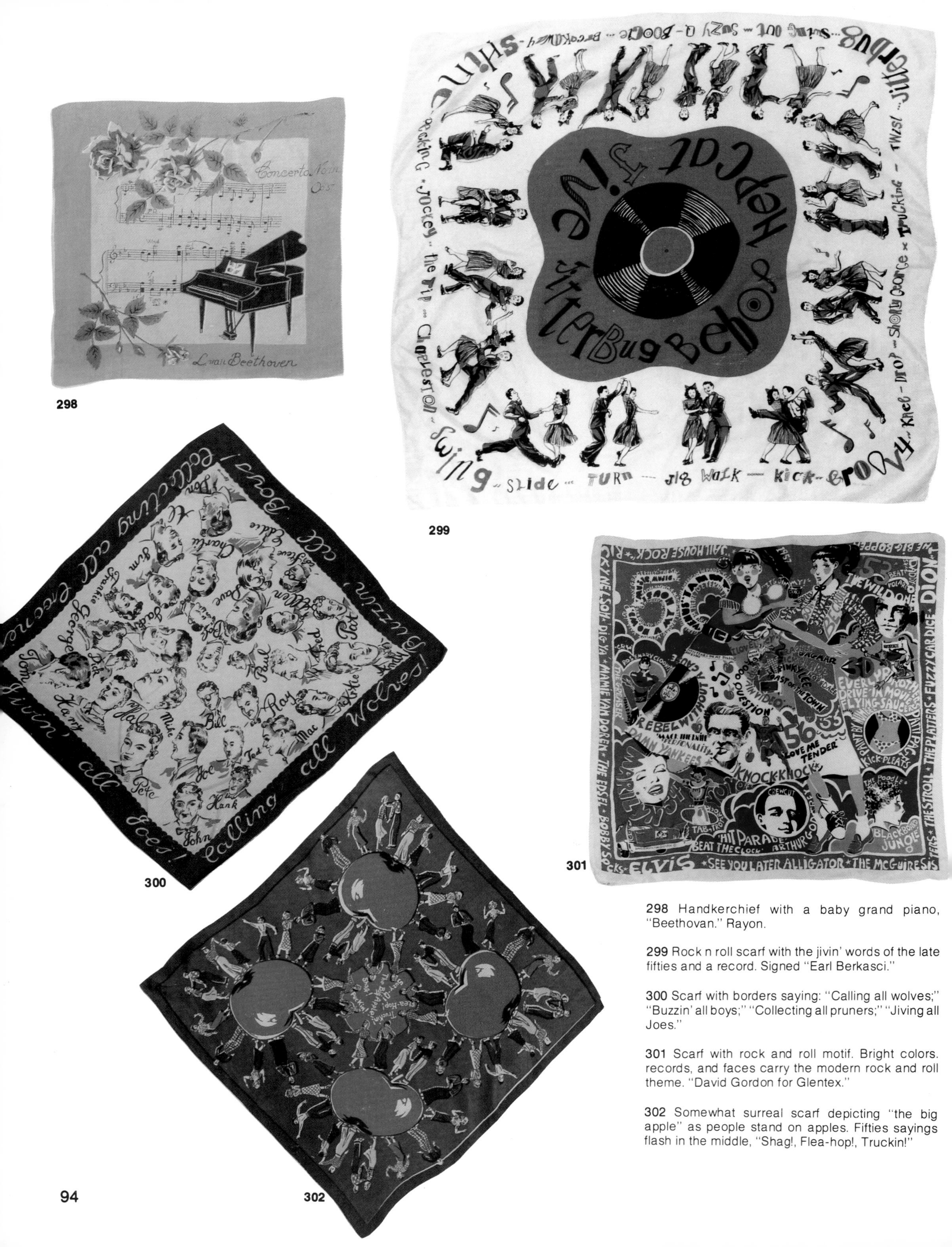

298 Handkerchief with a baby grand piano, "Beethovan." Rayon.

299 Rock n roll scarf with the jivin' words of the late fifties and a record. Signed "Earl Berkasci."

300 Scarf with borders saying: "Calling all wolves;" "Buzzin' all boys;" "Collecting all pruners;" "Jiving all Joes."

301 Scarf with rock and roll motif. Bright colors. records, and faces carry the modern rock and roll theme. "David Gordon for Glentex."

302 Somewhat surreal scarf depicting "the big apple" as people stand on apples. Fifties sayings flash in the middle, "Shag!, Flea-hop!, Truckin!"

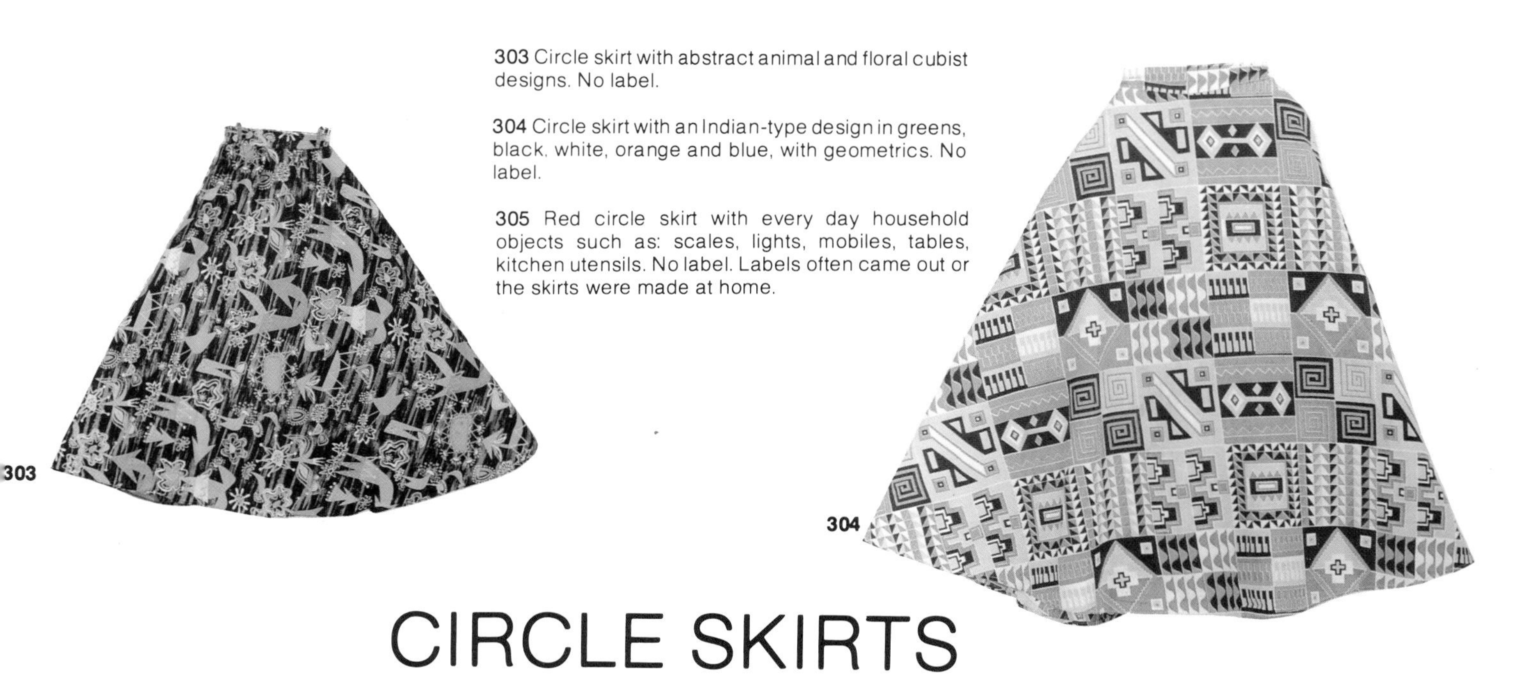

303 Circle skirt with abstract animal and floral cubist designs. No label.

304 Circle skirt with an Indian-type design in greens, black, white, orange and blue, with geometrics. No label.

305 Red circle skirt with every day household objects such as: scales, lights, mobiles, tables, kitchen utensils. No label. Labels often came out or the skirts were made at home.

CIRCLE SKIRTS

Pony tails and circle skirts entered the scene in America in the 1950s.

306 Black felt circle skirt with flamenco dancers. Label reads, "Julie Lynne, Charlot California."

307 Natives adorn this "Peerless Sportswear" cotton skirt.

308 Black felt circle skirt with ethnic dancers in blue and gold jumping across the skirt. The figures are similar to those seen on the fabrics. No label.

309 The funky hobo skirt made of cotton.

311

312

307

313

310

310 Shorter black cotton circle skirt with marionettes. No label.

311 Fabulous circle skirt with Mexican dancer motif. Rayon. Label reads, "Madalyn Miller Original, Los Angeles, Calif."

312 Circus motif on a black felt circle skirt with assorted animals, clowns and a poodle. No label.

313 Hand painted cotton skirt with native women carrying fruit on their heads. Their skirts actually lift up, and they go all around the skirt each with a lifting skirt. Label reads, "The California Slack Shops, Atlantic City, NJ."

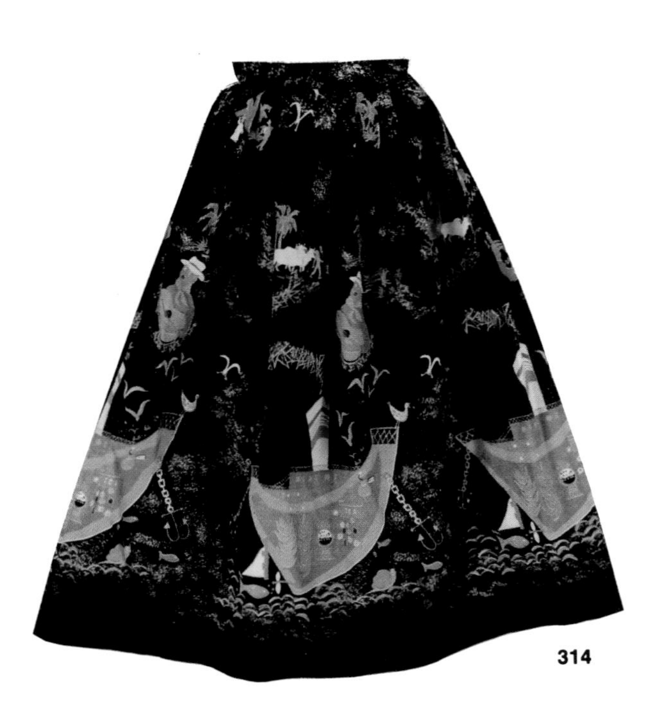

314

315

316

317

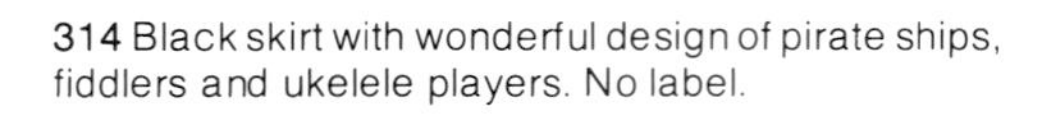

314 Black skirt with wonderful design of pirate ships, fiddlers and ukelele players. No label.

315 A-line skirt says "Around the world by Pan American Clipper." Scenes from around the world show the Eiffel Tower, Dutch wooden shoes, and a bull fight. No label.

316 Comical skirt with a cowboy holdup scene and a couple in car with hollywood glasses and the word, Rondavoo. "Tin horn Holiday, Never misbehaves" written on bottom. Has shirt to match.

317 Whimsical merry-go-round black cotton skirt. No label.

318

319

320

321

318 Stylized Egyptian motif on a black background, cotton. No label.

319 Circle skirt with a primitive Picasso-like design of multi-colored masks. The more colors used, the more expensive it is to manufacture. No label.

320 Vacation skirt, makes you want to jump right in! People in the 1950s had more money than in earlier decades and could afford to think about a vacation at the beach. Label reads, "An Original Casual. Casual Times of California."

321 Square patterned circle skirt with abstract faces or figures in each square.

322

322 Pink giraffes and trees on a black cotton circle skirt. No label.

323 Black circle skirt with brillaint appliquéd tropical fish in red, yellow, blue and hot pink.

324 Cotton flannel circle skirt with large decorative flying roosters of blue, gold and white.

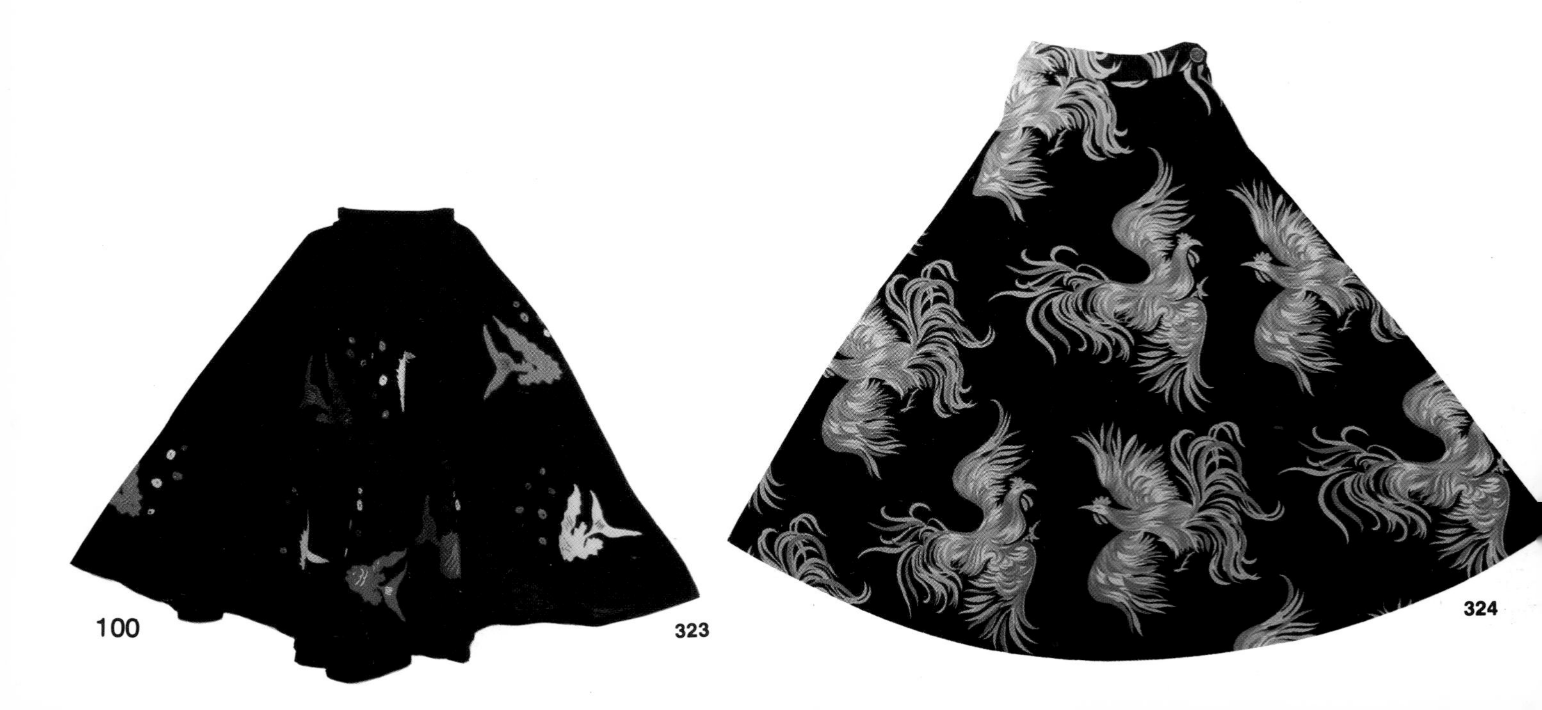

323

324

325 Fighting cocks on black background. No label.

326 Circle skirt covered in a whale design. No label.

327 Nifty black felt circle skirt with leopard cat, a Madalyn Miller Original, Los Angeles.

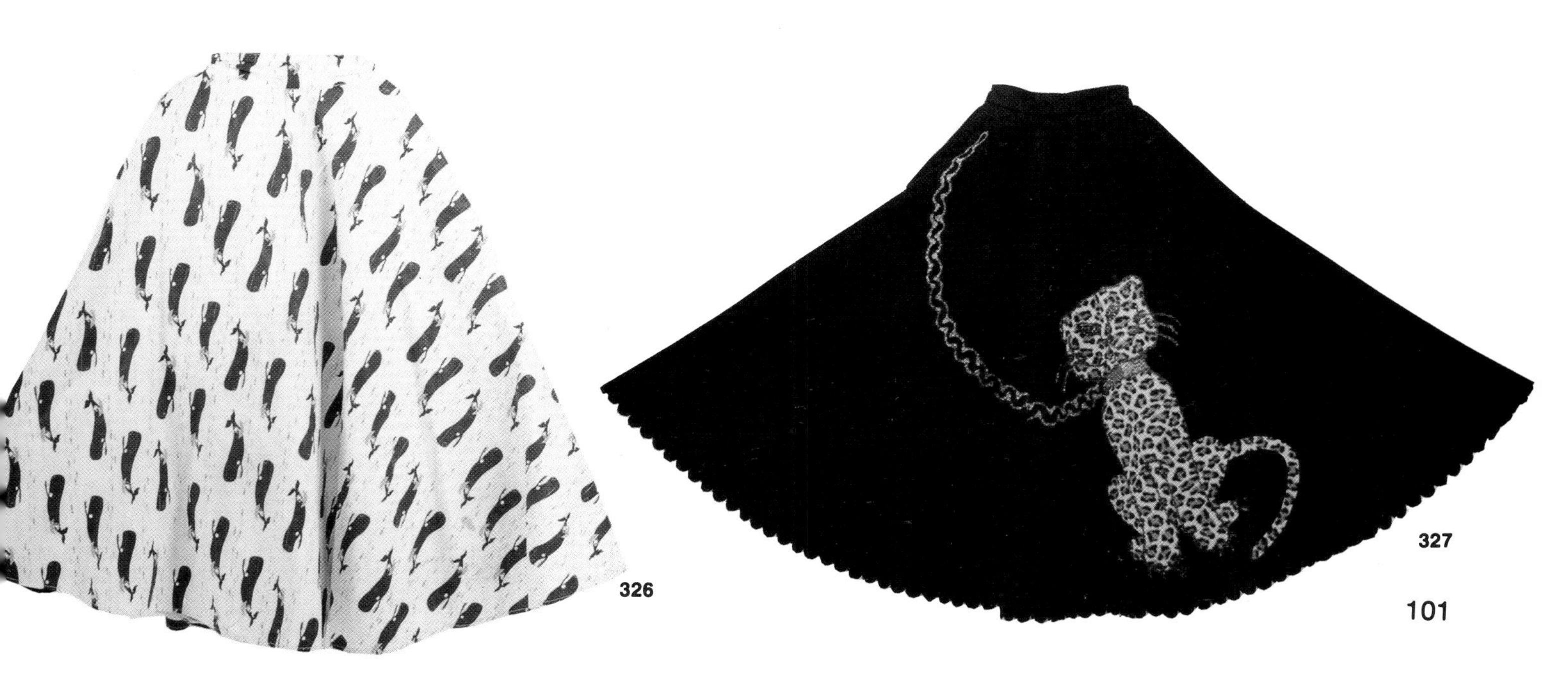

328 Beautiful floral appliqué circle skirt with roses on a black background. No label.

329 Fabulous abstract art design on a white background. Black, yellow, red, green, boomerangs and other abstract shapes adorn the skirt.

330 Black skirt with megaphones, camera, book and other various objects. No label.

331 Black felt circle skirt with large gold pineapples. Label reads, "La Boutique de Jeanne Lanvin, Castillo."

332 White cotton canvas circle skirt with watermellon, wine, flowerpot, barbeque utensils, and other household items. Label reads, "Ann Kelly of California, Los Angeles."

333

GABARDINE JACKETS

333 Blue thunderbird pattern on a dark blue jacket. Label reads, "Nelco-Built Sportswear Size 44."

334 Pink, grey and black jacket with the thunderbird pattern across the front yoke. Label reads, "Lake Sportswear Size 38."

334

335 Black and white American Indian pattern. The white part is tiny raised painted dots. Label reads, "Weather pressed jackets by Rissman Brothers."

336 An unusual yoke print on this beige fifties jacket.

337 Pink and black American Indian pattern. Label reads, "Canvas Outerwear, Size 42."

338 Funky looking grey and white American Indian style pattern. No label.

339

340

341

342

339 Peach, grey, black and white American Indian pattern. Reversible to solid peach. No label.

340 A series of geometric triangles or teepees decorate the yoke of this white gabardine jacket, giving an American Indian effect. Label reads, "Sport Chief by Chief Apparel Inc. New York. Size 38."

341 Red American Indian pattern on this gabardine jacket. Red is a rare color in the fifties. Four colors are used in this jacket. Size 44 is a large size and therefore very desirable among collectors.

342 American Indian pattern, or just a snowflake pattern decorates this brown gabardine jacket. Reversible.

343

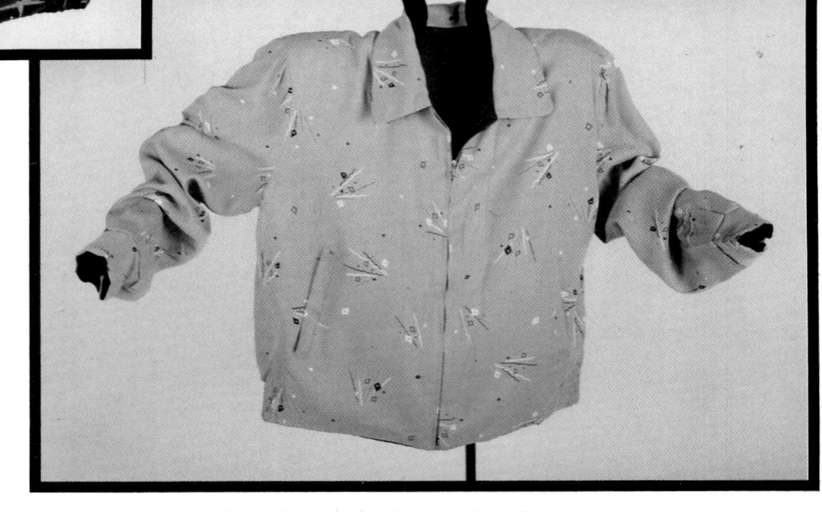

344

Gabardine jackets, otherwise known as "Eisenhower" or zip-up "waist length" jackets, were generally a late forties phenomenon that lasted throughout the fifties. The longer collars denote the forties style, whereas the jackets popular in the fifties had shorter collars. The old saying, "they don't make things the way they used to" certainly prevails when discussing the fabulous gabardine of the forties and fifties. The material is simply not available today, any collector will tell you. Pick up a piece of gabardine and feel the silky, heavy, draping material that holds such a rich quality.

345

343 Bold abstract linear print on a chocolate brown gabardine. Reversible.

344 Pale blue jacket with navy, orange and white in an atomic print. The jacket is reversible to bright navy.

345 A star-studded, non-reversible jacket in brown, white, gold.

346 Snowflake with skiers and Christmas trees. Label reads, "Sport Chief Snowflake."

347 Black, pink and blue rock 'n roll print gabardine jacket. Label reads, "Welgrune Size 44."

348 The snowflake jacket, with a yoke of skiiers. Label reads, "Sport Chief Snowflake."

349 Dark and light blue, black and white reversible abstract line print. No label. With hand tacking on collar.

350 Stars seem to be very popular on gabardine jackets. Label reads, "Nelco-Built Sportswear Size 42."

351 This grey and pink star studded jacket is reversible to solid pink.

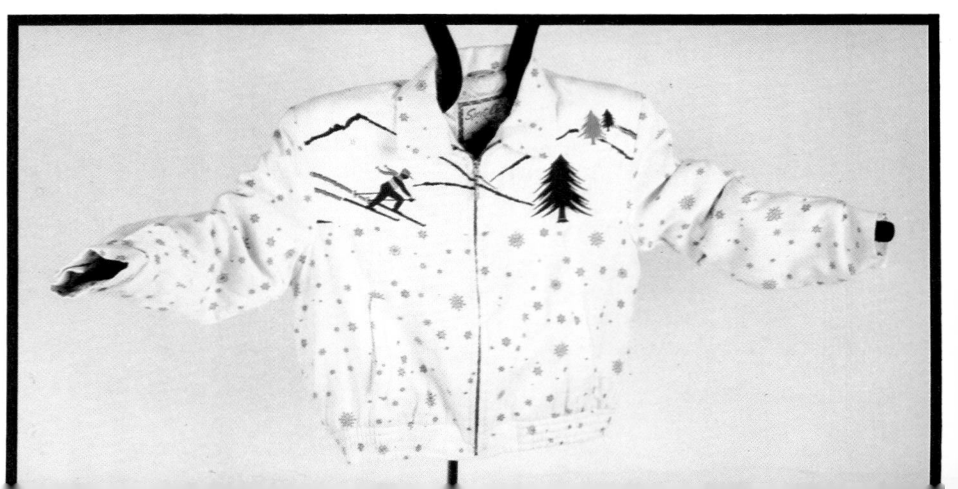

346

347

348

349

350

351

352

353

354

355

356

357

358 Short-sleeved boy-next-door shirt in white with blue collar and pocket trim.

359 Turquoise corduroy jacket with zebra cut-outs. Label reads, "Park Regal Sportswear, Buffalo, NY."

360 "Elvis Presley" style jacket, blue, white and navy with pleats. "Eton Hall Sportswear. Tailored on 5th Ave."

361 A rust, black and white unlined jacket, Elvis Presley style, with pleats and hand tacking. Label reads, "Hal Marshall in Miami. Size Medium."

358

360

359

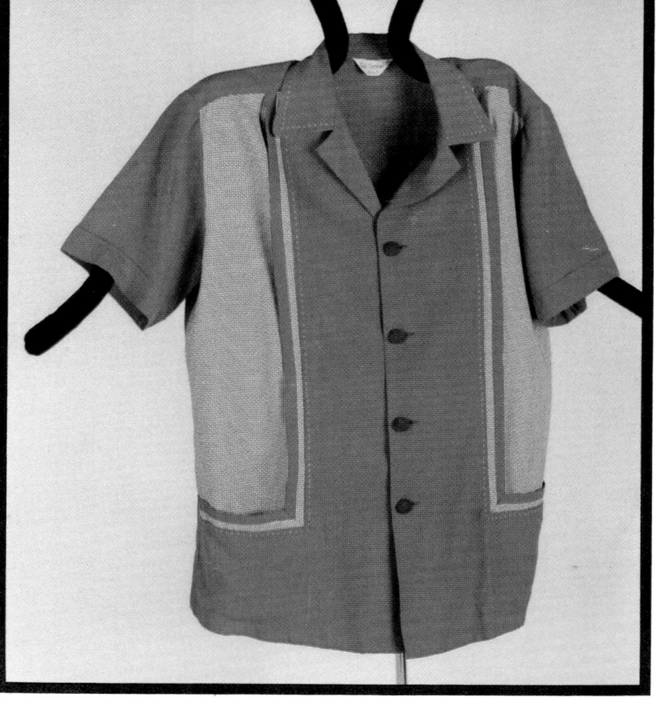

361

352 Black zippered jacket, with collar and front panels made from a white and tan geometric print. Label reads, "Styled Sportswear."

353 Black jacket with pink trim on the collar and on stitch-trimmed pockets. No label.

354 Black Fifties jacket with front panels of pale pink.

355 Black and pink checked rock 'n roll jacket. Label reads, "Buck Skein Brand."

356 This print gives a somewhat cellestial appeal. Label reads, "Fosterwear, Style by Lon Foster."

357 Black and white ski jacket with a sunburst-look yoke. No label.

ROCK 'N ROLL SHIRTS

362 Black and white gabardine with striped panels and assymetrical striped insets. Label reads, "Campus."

363 Grey men's gabardine pleated pants with zebra side pleats, pockets and matching belt. "Styled by J. Morein, Philadelphia."

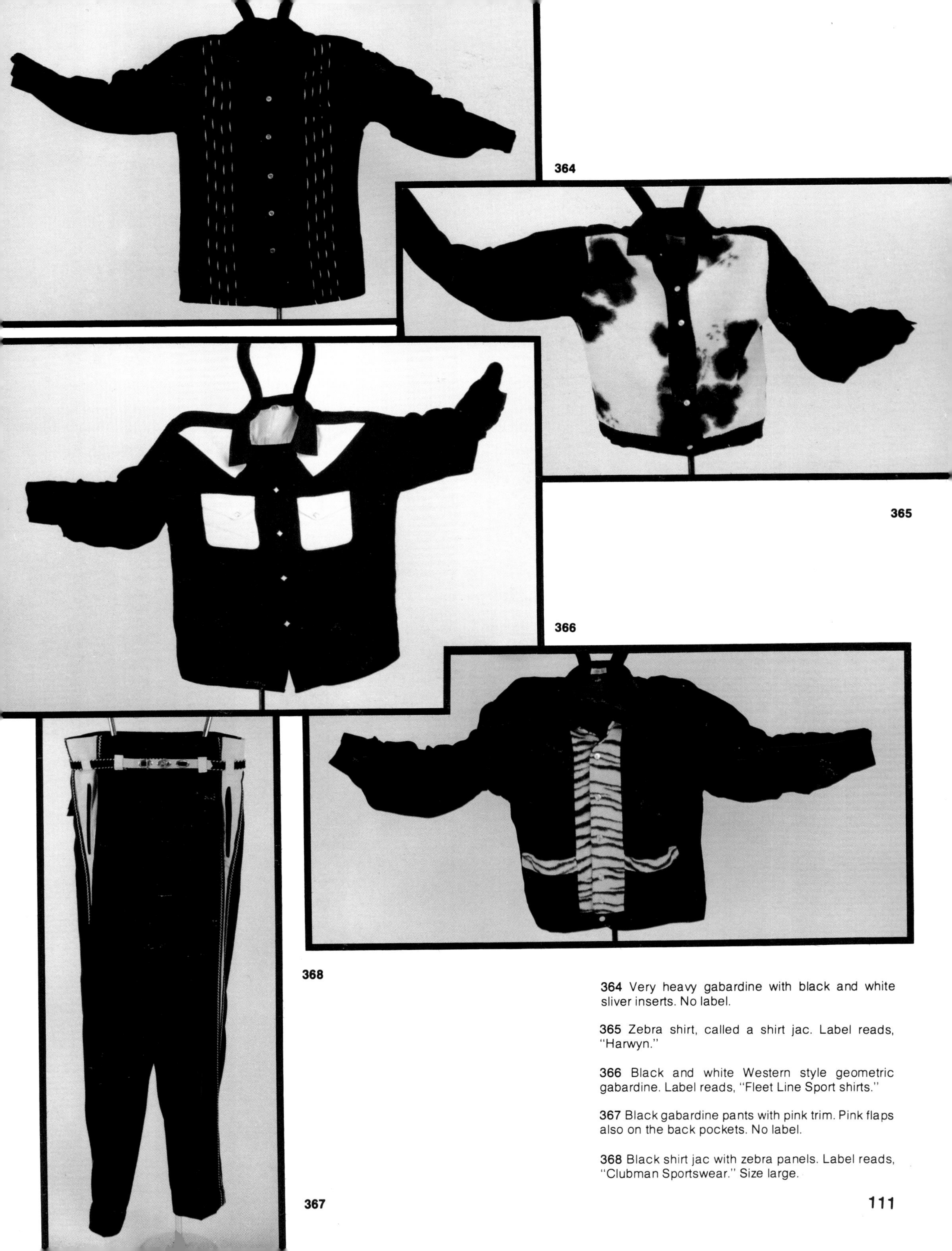

364

365

366

368

367

364 Very heavy gabardine with black and white sliver inserts. No label.

365 Zebra shirt, called a shirt jac. Label reads, "Harwyn."

366 Black and white Western style geometric gabardine. Label reads, "Fleet Line Sport shirts."

367 Black gabardine pants with pink trim. Pink flaps also on the back pockets. No label.

368 Black shirt jac with zebra panels. Label reads, "Clubman Sportswear." Size large.

372 Red and grey gabardine jacket. Label reads, "Westward-Ho Sportswear by Gilman."

373 Dark green shirt with bold orange streaks.

374 Blue and black pop-art shirt. Label reads, "Marlboro." Size large.

369

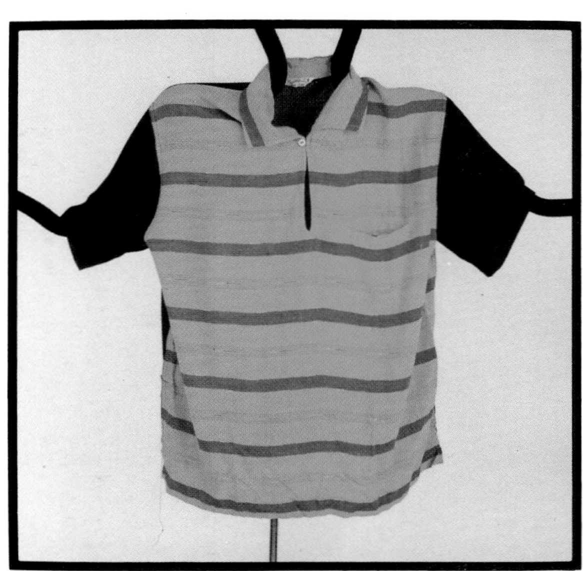

371

373

369 A great red gabardine shirt with white lamé panels. "Penny's Sportscraft."

370 The lightning bolt shirt. Label reads, "Sportop." Size large. Rayon.

371 Salmon and black striped shirt. Label reads, "Sportswear L hand washable."

374

The year 1954 denotes a turning point in America as people saw the downfall of Senator Joseph R. McCarthy, the desegregation of schools, the introduction of powerful, tail-finned cars, and the emergence of an innovative, urgent unique kind of pop music—soon to be known as "rock and roll."

The "rock" culture brought with it a whole new craze in fashion as well as a completely new language. The fifties saw the emergence of the color pink, which before had been restricted to women's lingerie, popping up on menswear mixed with charcoal grey or black. You were square if you didn't have a poodle skirt or an Elvis Presley hairdo. The creation of rock 'n' roll and such entertainers as Chuck Berry, Billie Holiday and Elvis Presley turned the teenage years around. Their influence has become a permanent fixture in American popular culture. Music became the chosen medium of revolt for the young in the fifties. Musical notes themselves became motifs of decorative art at this time.

375

376

375 Brown geometric triangle shirt. Gabardine with blue and white. Label reads, "Lancer made in California." Large.

376 Rock 'n roll shirt, red with white pleats and black glittery fabric. Label reads, "Bud Berma Originals."

377

379

377 This shirt really looks as if it was painted, as if it is all brush strokes.

378 Turquoise and black gabardine pull-over. Label reads, "Sportwear." Size Large.

379 Wonderful black gabardine shirt with salmon and grey squiggle squares. No label.

380

380 Black gabardine shirt with pink and turquoise stripes in a hand painted effect. Label reads, "Sea Island." Size Large.

381 Grey gabardine shirt with pink collar with black and white tiny hearts. The flap on the top of the pocket also has tiny hearts in pink. "Styled in Italy for Canvas." Size large.

382 Men's ivory and black gabardine pants. "Created and Manufactured by J. Morein."

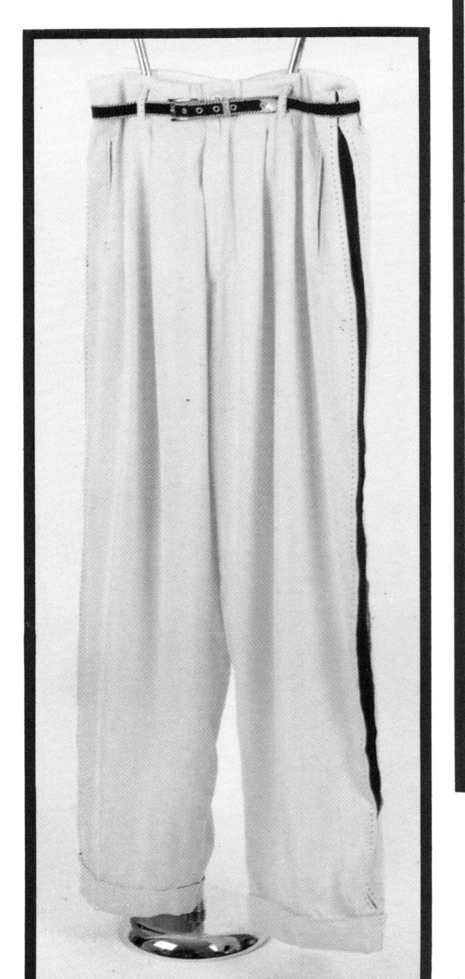

382

383

384

385

383 Men's pink gabardine pants with black trim on the sides and the back pockets. No label.

84 A true Rock 'n roll shirt made of heavy gabardine with pink and black pleats and pink hand tacking with pink mother-of-pearl buttons. Label reads, "Gaucho Originals Styled in Hollywood." Size large.

385 If this isn't fifties, I don't know what is, a pink and black panel shirt. No label.

386 Men's gabardine pink and black pants. "Styled and manufactured by J. Morein of Philadelphia."

387 Bubble shirt in lavendar, black and white. Label reads, "Shirt craft."

386

387

PRINT SHIRTS

389

Many may not know this, but Hawaiian shirts were introduced by Missionaries to the Hawaiian natives in the 1800s. Of course, it was not the Hawaiian shirt as we know it today, but it was the same boxy, oversize short-sleeved style. They were introduced to the natives as a comfortable, loose-fitting garb to cover their nakedness. The natives transformed the shirt into the wild, festive shirt that we know today. The Hawaiians hand-painted plain shirts with colorful depictions of their environment, with such images as hibiscus flowers, pineapples, fish, volcanoes and surfers.

The shirts were imported into America when servicemen returned from World War II. Hollywood strengthened the craze for the shirts with such movies as *From Here to Eternity*. Even President Truman donned one on the cover of *Time* magazine in 1951.

Ellery J. Chun is credited with coining the term "aloha shirt" and with being the first to commercially manufacture them in 1936. He sought to produce ready-to-wear shirts for tourists who couldn't wait several days to have one tailormade. The name of Chun's store, King-Smith is featured as the "creator" of the term, aloha shirt. Another innovator in the field was George Brangier who started Branfleet, which later became Kahala Sportswear in 1936. By the 1950s, aloha or Hawaiian shirts were an international fashion rage.

Originally, and until the late 1920s, the shirts were made from cotton or silk fabric. But in 1924, these shirts were made from the old rayon by the DuPont Company. This rayon, a wood cellulose product, took dyes beautifully and was even finer than silk. In the mid-1950s, a fire at the DuPont factory destroyed the original rayon recipe. The old rayon was much softer, giving the shirts the nickname, "silkies." The shirts made prior to the fire are much more collectible. To decipher whether a shirt is a true classic, look for double-stitched seams, long collar points, and sleeves that drape naturally. Bill Cosby, Steven Spielberg and Robin Williams are among those devoted to collecting the truely classic Hawaiian shirts, either as kitsch or as true folk art. Shirts that once sold for a buck in the 1930s now sell for several hundred times the original price.

390

388 Ameoba-like shapes. Label reads, "The Kahala made in Honolulu. Eva-Jon Hawaiian Shop. La Jolla." Size large.

389 Blue shirt with patterns of yellow, white and red. "Catalina, A California Creation, Los Angeles, California." Size Large.

390 A winner for the Fourth of July, this black shirt is ablaze with stars and flares of red, green and yellow.

391

391 Red, black and white squiggle shirt. Squiggles form large floral type patterns. "Duke Champion Kahanamoku a Hawaiian Original." (earlier label). Size large.

392 Large shaded leaves with black, white and grey shaded patterns. "Malihini, made in Hawaii." Large.

393 Abstract pattern of houses and palm trees. "Hollywood Sportswear by Blenheim." Size Large.

392

393

394

395

396

397

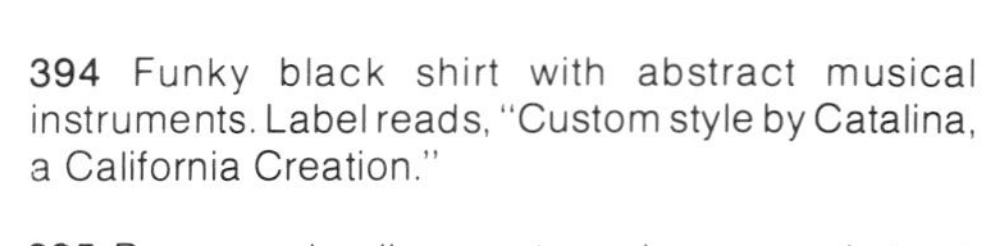

394 Funky black shirt with abstract musical instruments. Label reads, "Custom style by Catalina, a California Creation."

395 Brown and yellow spots make up an abstract jungle motif. Label reads, "Manhattan." Size M/L.

396 Geometric triangles. "Cali-Fane of Los Angeles." Large.

397 Abstract spear fisherman. "Blocks Southland Sportswear." Medium large.

398 Corduroy, grey, orange, white and blue. American Indian, similar to Chief's blanket "Penney's Towncraft Size large."

399 Corduroy American Indian pattern shirt, red, blue, black and white. A famous label hangs inside, "Penney's Towncraft Size Large."

400 Olive green with orange and black, this shirt is decorated with patterns and masks reminiscent of the ancient Aztecs.

401 Red corduroy shirt with African masks and stripes. Marked, "Wesley." Size large.

402 A bold checkerboard yoke decorates this bright red shirt.

403 Dark grey corduroy shirt with American Indian multi-colored yoke. Label reads, "Brent Montgomery Ward Size large."

404

404 Cotton shirt with an Africanesque motif on a yellow background. Label reads, "The Pilgrim Sportswear."

405 Red and blue Hawaiian shirt with Africanesque figures in turquoise squares. "Tailored by Art Vogue in California." Size large.

405

406

407

409

408

411

410

406 A pale green Fifties shirt with primitive drum and spear motif. Marked "Made in Hawaii for Waikiki Shop Pompano Beach Florida."

407 Rayon Hawaiian with primitive motif-Hawaiian. "Tropicana made in Honolulu Hawaii" grey background.

408 Rock 'n roll shirt with an interesting African motif along the front. Label reads, "Bud Berma Originals. New slotted collar with removable stays." Rayon.

409 Hawaiian shirt with abstract motifs. "Made in Hawaii." Rayon Crepe as opposed to the silkie rayon.

410 Black cotton shirt with African Tom Toms. Label reads, "Arrow Made in USA Sanforized Reg. US Pat.Off. Size M/L."

411 Rayon shirt with African primitive motif. Label reads, "Hollywood Rambler, Made in California."

413

412 Rows of hieroglyphs cover this shirt, in vivid colors clearly never faded by the scorching Egyptian sun.

413 Hawaiian shirt with a combination of palm trees and American Indian pattern, with chocolate brown, chartreuse, red, emerald green and flesh-color. Famous Hawaiian shirt label, "Duke Champion Kahanamoku. Made by Cisco." The most prolific of labels, they made great stuff. You can tell this is an early fifties shirt by the collar.

414 Wonderful, cotton American Indian pattern. Label reads, "Custom style by Catalina, California Creations." Size large.

415 Cotton, definitely 1940s with long collar. "The Champ of Hollywood, Made in California." All-over American Indian pattern. Multi-colored.

416 American Indian pattern shirt. Label reads 'Club Man. Imported Yarn, unconditionally washable." Rayon.

414

415

6

417

418

419

420

417 Black, pink and white gabardine shirt with an American Indian influence. Label reads, "Pilgrim. Sears Roebuck and Co. USA Size Large."

418 Lime green all-over pattern of tiny Indians. Label reads, "The Riviera Sandy MacDonald."

419 Brown, blue and black American Indian pattern fifties shirt. Label reads, "Sandy MacDonald." Rayon.

420 Over-all American Indian Sante Fe pattern from "Miamian Sportswear by Aetna."

421 American Indian pattern shirt. Label reads, "Wesley Medium." Pale blue.

422 Red, white and blue snowflake ski shirt. Label reads, "Unwood Sportswear."

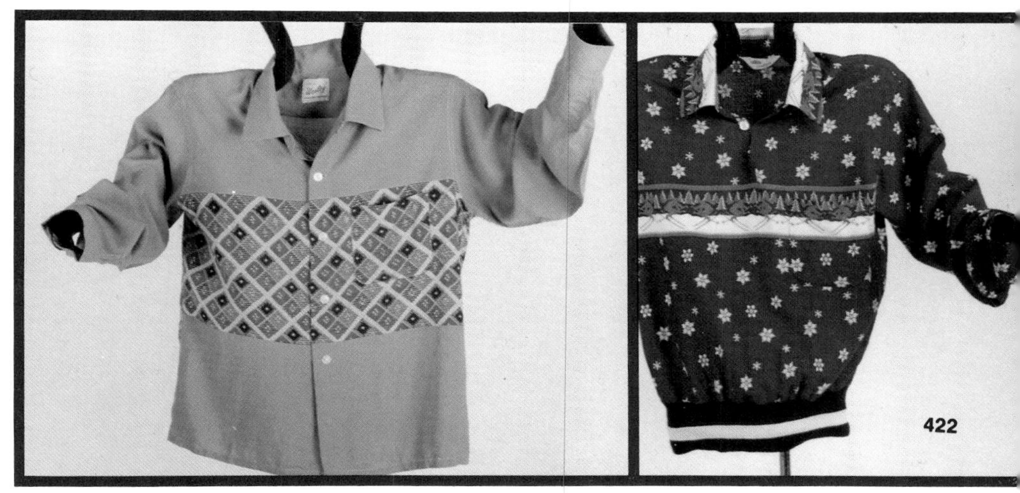

421

422

423

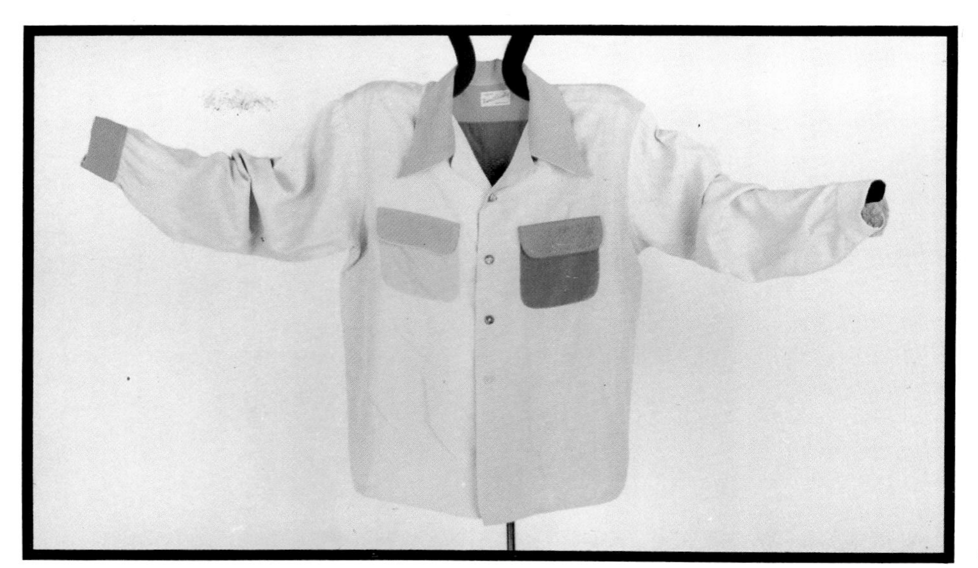
424

423 This hand painted shirt is similar to the hand painted ties. "Alexander of Hollywood, California."

424 End of day patchwork style shirt.

425

426

427

425 A corduroy shirt with black and white chess board print, and chess figures making up the yoke. Label reads, "Penney's Towncraft, Size large."

426 Gabardine pull-over with snowflake pattern. Label reads, "Sportswear." Size Large.

427 Black zebra shirt. "Aloha Kanaka Original by Art Wogur."

431

428 A tangerine dream in Rayon with a black, white and yellow line pattern. Label reads "Arrow." Size Medium.

429 Squiggle patterned shirt with black backgroun and geometric squares and squiggles. Label reads "Montelito of California."

430 Peach shirt with black, white and grey squiggles No label. Size Large.

431 Gray rayon squiggle shirt with atomic pattern No label.

432 True scribble shirt. Label reads, "Mullen Bluet Los Angeles Sportswear." Large.

433

434

435

436

437

433 1950s atomic print, in a rayon gabardine. Label reads, "Wesley."

434 Fabulous rayon gabardine shirt with grey, turquoise and yellow design. The design reminds one of Mondrian or Klee. No label.

435 50s with primitive stick figures. Tropicana made in Honolulu, Hawaii. Size large.

436 Peach shirt with black, white and grey squiggles. No label. Size Large.

437 Yellow gabardine with grey bulls eyes. Label reads, "Penny's Towncraft."

438

439

440

438 Back panel shirt in black with boy blowing a conch shell. "Pacific Sportswear made in Hawaii."

439 Back panel shirt in black known as "the volcano shirt." "Surf riders Sportswear, Made in Honolulu Hawaii." Size Large.

440 Hawaiian outfit, shirt and shorts in black and orange. "Duke Champion, Kahanamoku made by Cisco."

441

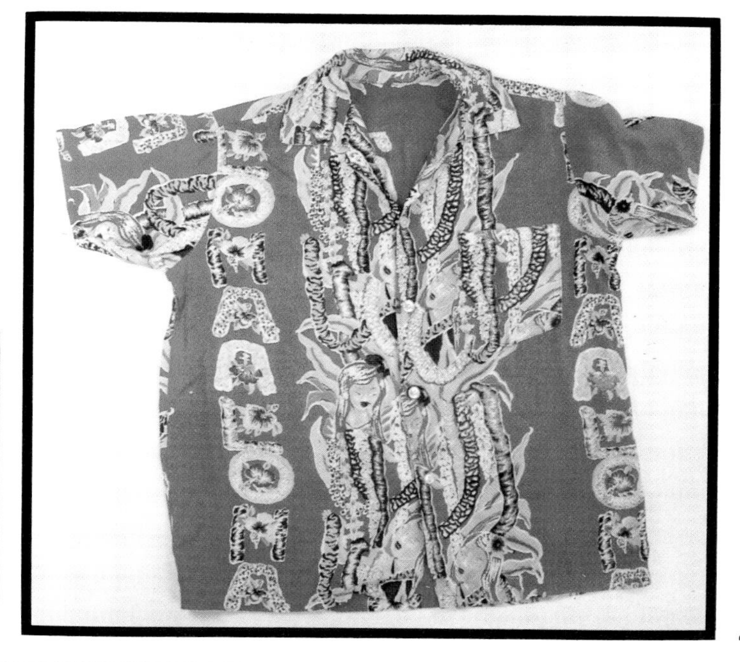

443

442

441 Hawaiian shirt, back panel shirt with Hawaiian woman on back, red. To its left,the front panel. with floralp[ockets and collar. Label reads "Capistrano by Wismar made in California Size large."

442 Child's red Hawaiian shirt. No label.

443 A typical Hawaiian motif with boats and luau with a geometric and squiggle background. Label reads, "Hale Hawaii."

444 A geometric Hawaiian shirt with palm trees in circular designs. Label reads, "Kohanomoku."

444a Woman's Hawaiian shirt covered with sushi carts and the words "Barbeque and Sushi." No label.

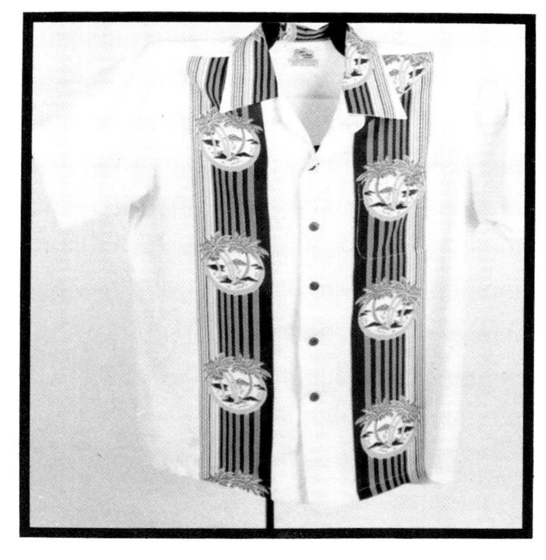

444

444a

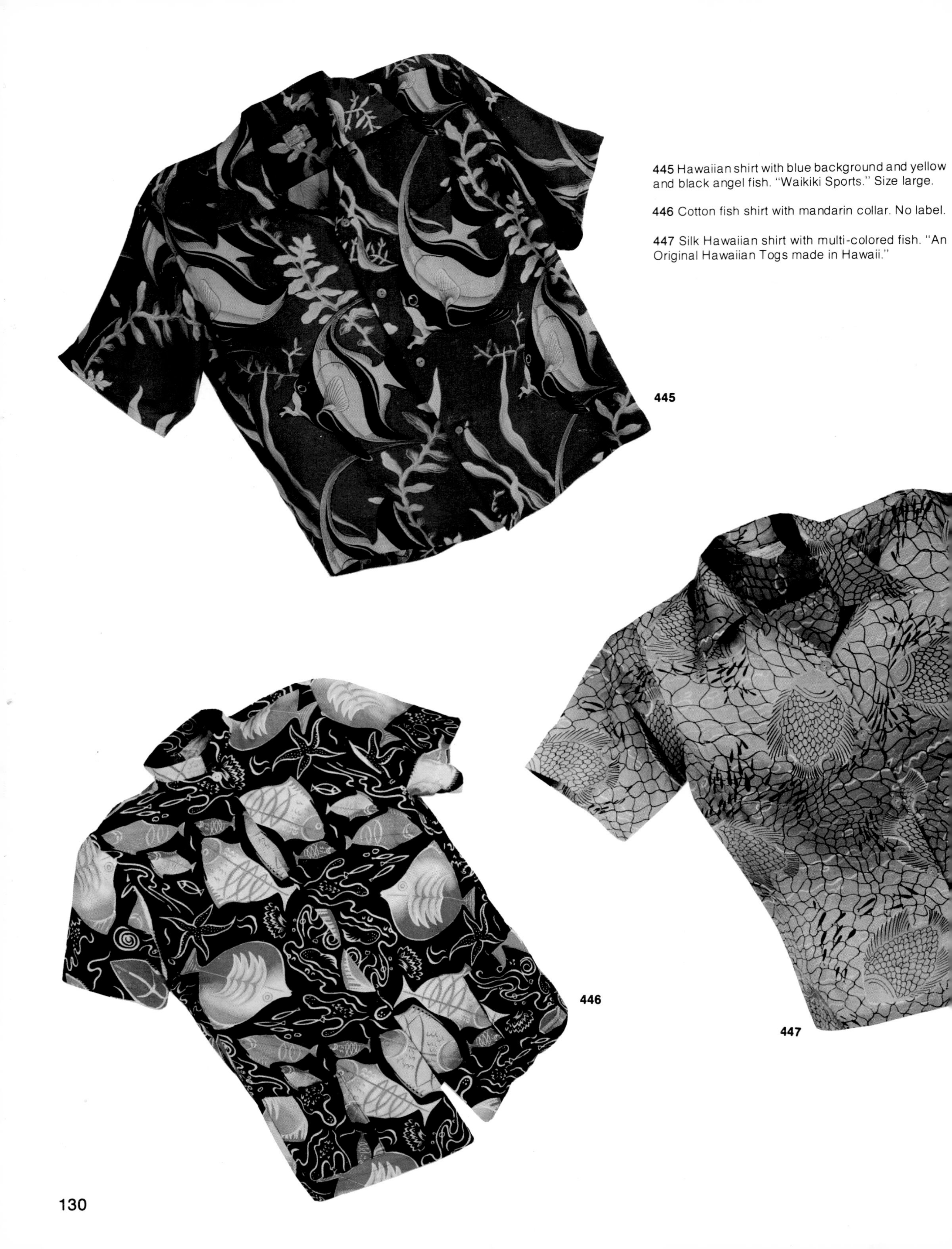

445 Hawaiian shirt with blue background and yellow and black angel fish. "Waikiki Sports." Size large.

446 Cotton fish shirt with mandarin collar. No label.

447 Silk Hawaiian shirt with multi-colored fish. "An Original Hawaiian Togs made in Hawaii."

445

446

447

448

449

450

451

452

453

448 Rayon fish shirt in brown, chartreuse and burnt orange. "Catalina, a california creation and styled for the stars of Hollywood. Los Angeles, Calif."

449 Perrywinkle blue fish shirt. "Kamehameha."

450 The fisherman catching the mermaid, rayon pull-over. Label reads, "Distinctive Sportswear." Medium. Hand painted.

451 The seahorse shirt, Hawaiian, red. "Made in California." Size large.

452 The starfish shirt. No label. Black background.

453 Maroon fish shirt with chartreuse. "Surf 'n Sand made in Honolulu Hawaii." Size large.

454 Abstract fish shirt. "Surf 'n Sand made in Honolulu Hawaii." Large.

455 Underwater fish shirt with outerspace feeling. "Hale Hawaii," XL made in Hawaii.

455

454

456

458

457

459

461

460

462

456 Abstract underwater scene decorates this cotton shirt. Label reads, "Hawaiian Surf made in Hawaii." Size Large.

457 Wonderful abstract underwater scene with abstract fish. "Palomino California Sportswear." XL.

458 Hawaiian shirt. Abstract underwater scene with fish. Label reads, "Watumull's Honolulu."

459 The burnt orange swordfish Hawaiian shirt. "Duke Champion Kahanamoku made by Cisco."

460 The "bug eye fish shirt," Hawaiian. "Made in Hawaii by Kahala for Andrade Resort Shop Royal Hawaiian Hotel."

461 Cotton Hawaiian fish shirt. "Watumull's & Leilani made in Hawaii." Size large. White background with brown.

462 Shirt has fish from Hawaii with their names, a directory of Hawaiian fish. "Kaimana Hila Created by Hawaiian Philipinne Importand Export Co." Size Large.

463 Marlin swordfish shirt. Label reads, "Shaheen's of Honolulu." Size XL.

463

464

HAWAIIAN DRESSES

465

464 Hawaiian dress decorated with ukeleles and Hawaiian words. Label reads, "Shaheen's of Honolulu."

465 The shower curtain print with an abstract underwater scene. "Kamehameha."

466

466 Beautiful colors in this Hawaiian dress, it looks like a Gauguin-inspired print. Marked, "Kamehameha." Almost psychedelic looking.

467

467 Long rayon 1940s Hawaiian dress with train. The colors are earthy with green, black, white and red with a footprints pattern. Label reads, "Shaheen's of Honolulu."

468 Light blue Hawaiian dress which reads, "United Airlines, Nellie McGuire welcomes you." Label reads, "Tom McGuire. Surf riders, Made in Honolulu."

468

469 Rare label reads, "Holo-Holo, Honolulu." Shows all of the islands on the dress.

469

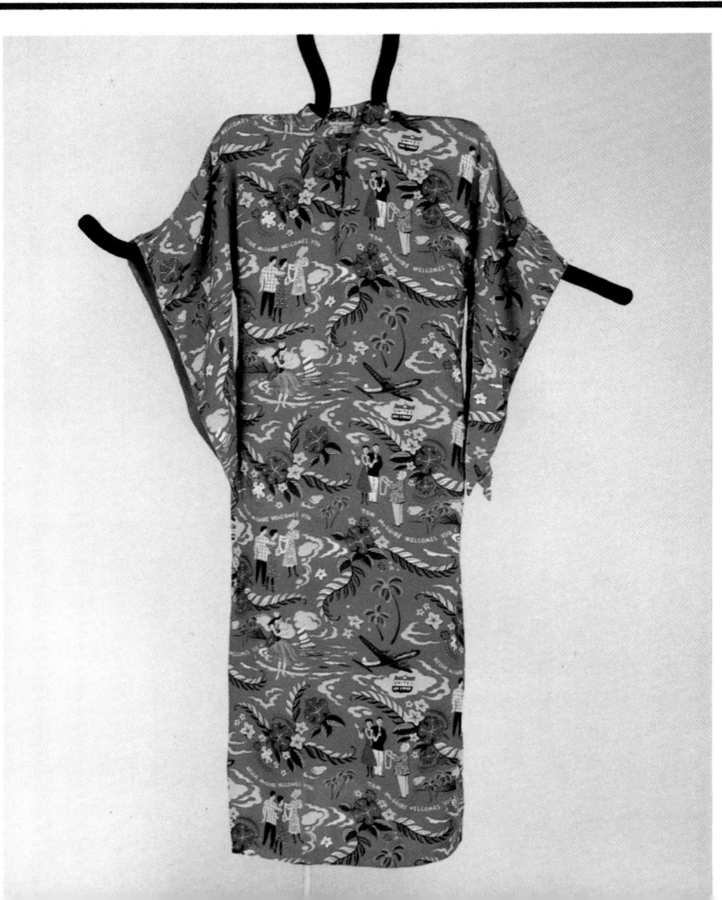

470

470 Floral Hawaiian dress. Label reads, "Kamehameha."

471

471 Hawaiian dress with an underwater scene. Label reads, "Royal Hawaiian made in Honolulu for The Liberty House."

472 Hawaiian dress with fringe collar with a landscape print with people, no label.

472

473 "Malihini Hale at Waikiki." Floral lais and ladies faces make this dress extremely interesting.

473

474

474 Lotus blossoms adorn this Hawaiian dress. Label reads, "Royal Hawaiian Quality Garments."

475 Surf riders and sailboats adorn this dress in a figural pattern.

475

477

476

478

476 Hawaiian dress in a rare salmon color. Marked, "Kamehameha, Made and styled in Hawaii."

477 The spear fishing dress. Label reads, "Tropicana made in Honolulu."

478 Sleeveless Hawaiian dress with an underwater print. Label reads, "Malihini made in Hawaii."

RAYON DRESSES

479 Black straight dress with winged lady. "Eisenberg Original."

480 Black and ivory vine pattern of grapes. "Eisenberg & Sons Original." Vine pattern appliqué in silver studs.

481 Hand painted Landscape with sheep and clouds.

482 Dress covered with pink flamingos.

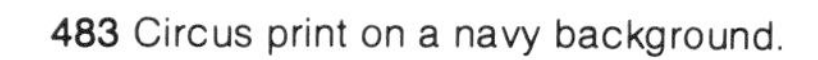

483 Circus print on a navy background.

484 Dress with scenes of Manhattan on a white background. No label.

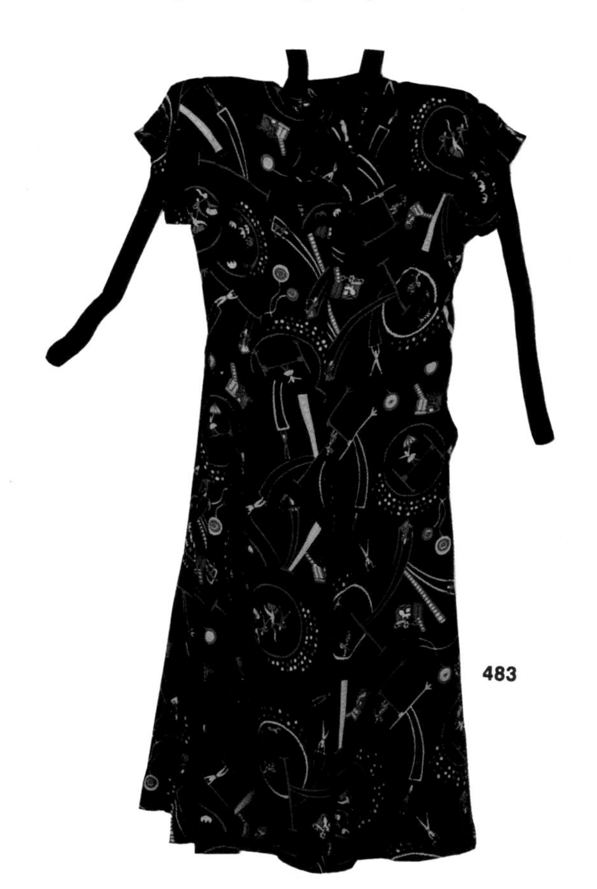

485

486

487

488

485 Green squiggle dress made of a light rayon. Label reads, "Fashioned by Form Fit Dresses. New York." Plastic buttons.

486 Black and white straight skirt with jacket. Label reads "Ann Koffman."

487 Black, white and red dress with jacket and abstract design. No label.

488 Green squiggle dress with Dennis the Menace spirals. No label.

489 Squiggle dress. Brown with splashed colors throughout. "Jackson Pollack style." Label reads, "Mode O'Day. Styled in California."

490 Brown dress with black design and fringe design on front. Beads at the center of each black star. No label.

492 Franz Kline-esque black and white patterned squiggle dress with velvet trim. Label reads "Suzy Perette."

493 Black dress. The seasons are listed in French in a circle with people being swirled away in them. also says directions in French, Est, Nord, Sud etc. with people. No label.

494 Straight dress with abstract design in various colors.

495 Burgundy dress with abstract floral design. No label.

490

492

493

494

France was no longer the leader of fashion after the war. This gave America the chance to find its own creativeness and step forward in the fashion industry. A relationship between fine art and applied art existed in fashion as well as in textiles and many rayon dresses exhibited the abstract expressionism of the popular textiles.

489

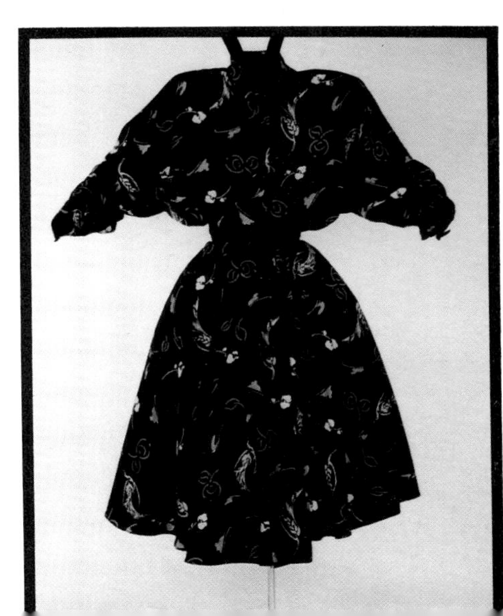

495

ROBES, SHORTS & TRUNKS

496 Red Hawaiian trunks, "The Kahala made in Honolulu for Bullock's."

497 Tan "Campus Sportswear" swim trunks with pocket in front and huge shark.

498 Forest green "Duke Champion Kohanamoku An Hawaiian Original" swim trunks.

499 Hawaiian motif by "McGregor."

500 Blue/Green Hawaiian motif trunks, "Campus Sportswear."

497

499

500

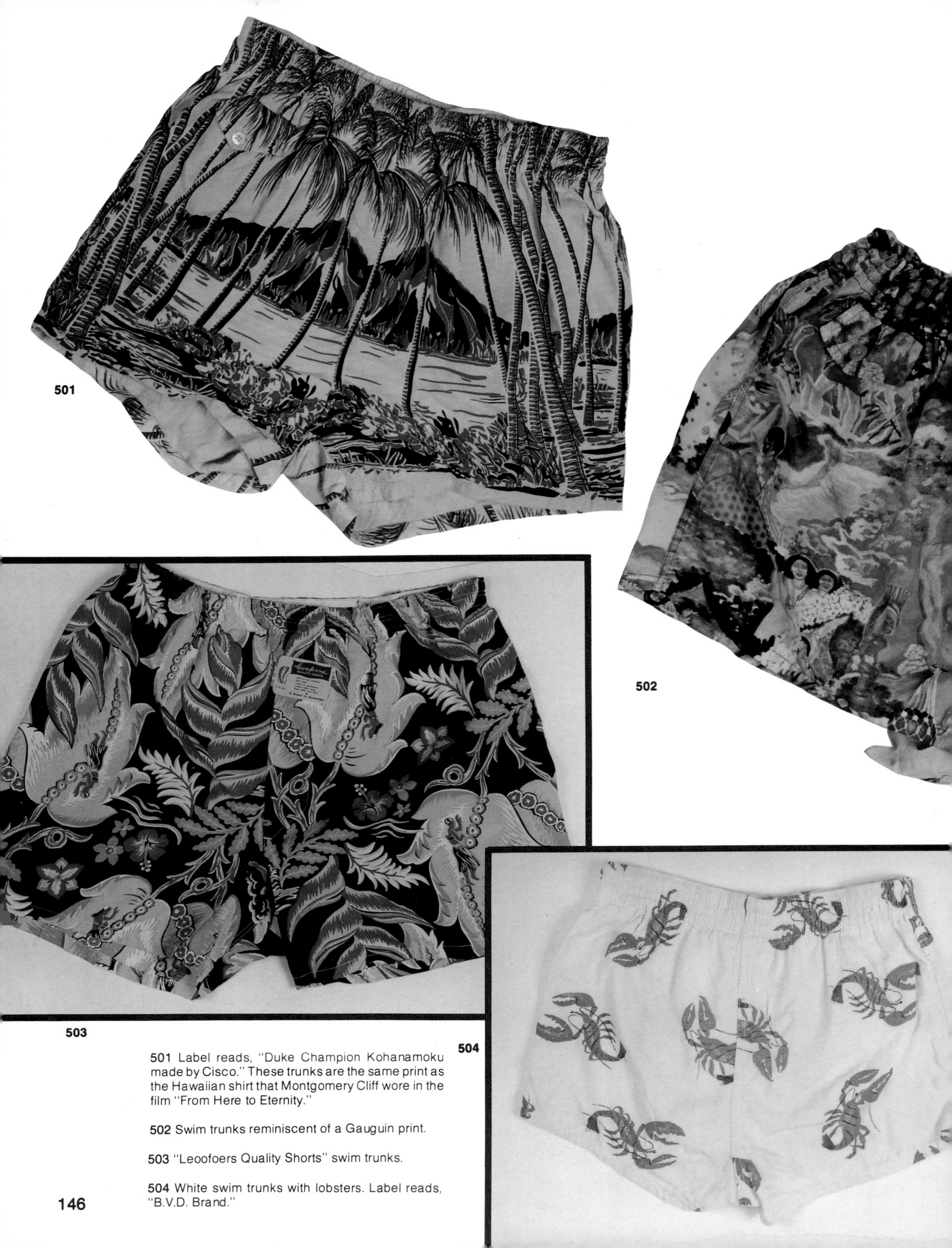

501

502

503

504

501 Label reads, "Duke Champion Kohanamoku made by Cisco." These trunks are the same print as the Hawaiian shirt that Montgomery Cliff wore in the film "From Here to Eternity."

502 Swim trunks reminiscent of a Gauguin print.

503 "Leoofoers Quality Shorts" swim trunks.

504 White swim trunks with lobsters. Label reads, "B.V.D. Brand."

505

506

507

505 Striped fish on these swim trunks. No label.

506 Hawaiian boxers with red background.

507 Pale yellow "McGregor Swim 'n Play" swim trunks. The Hawaiian surfer spruces them up a bit.

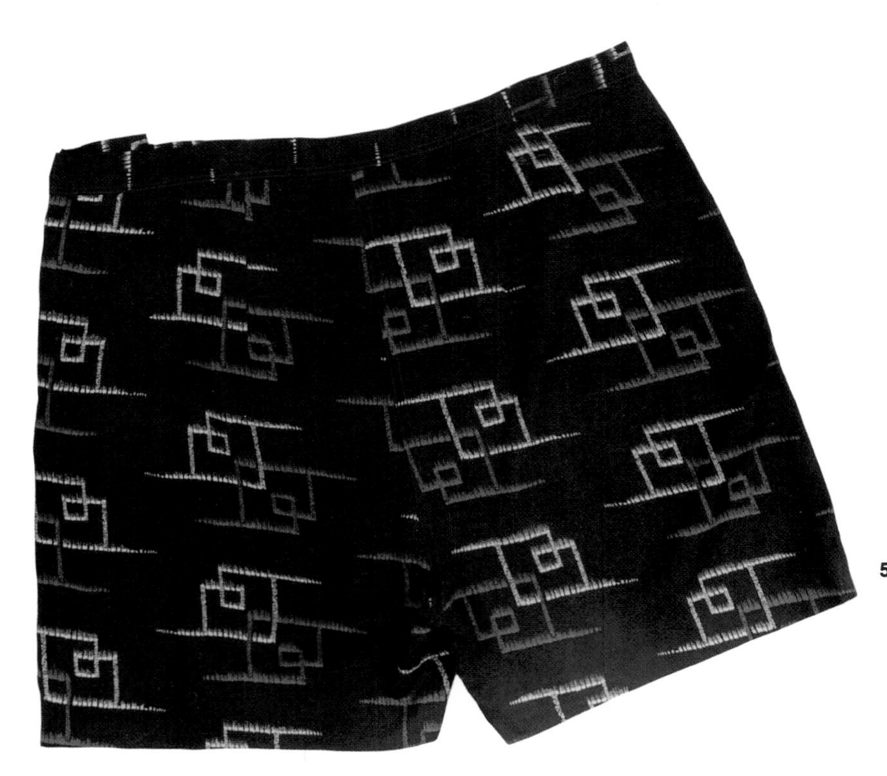

508

508 Blue swim trunks with orange and white geometric design pattern.

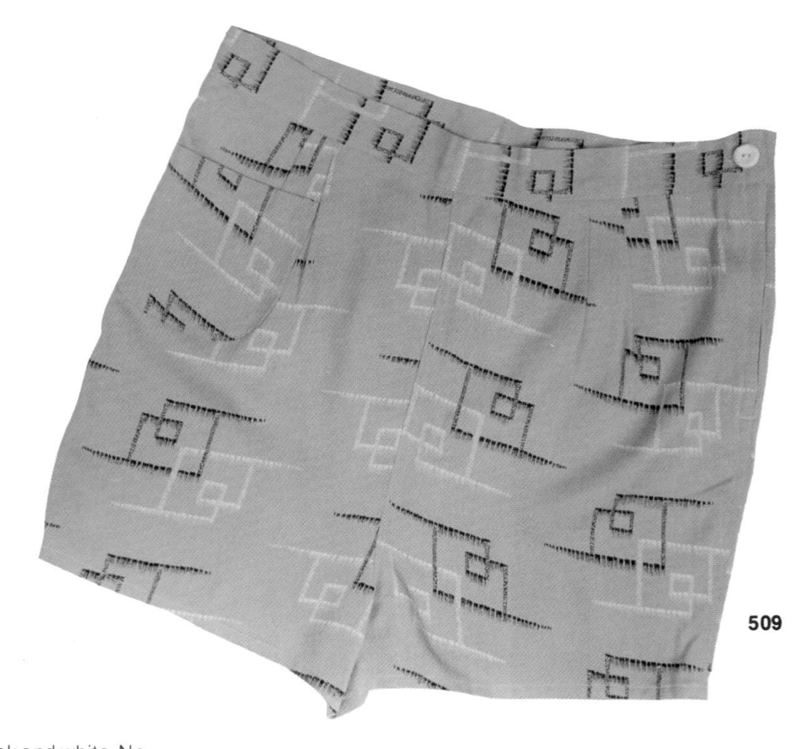

509

509 The same trunks in tan with black and white. No label.

510

510 Atomic abstract design of orange, green and white on dark green swim trunks. No label.

511

511 Grey with pink and white abstract design, very fifties. No label.

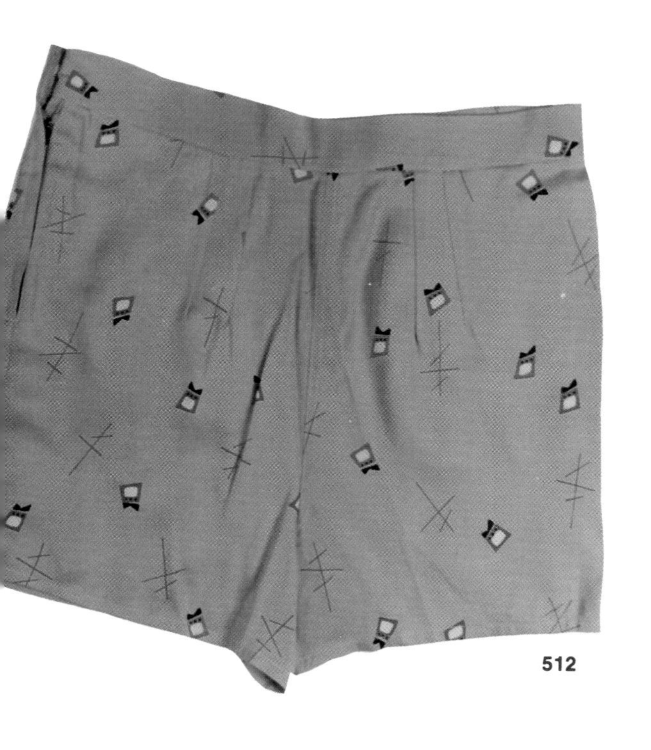

512

512 Tan trunks with orange and black television sets! No label.

513 Brightly colored geometric smoking jacket with black brim. No label.

514 Pink robe with black and white abstract design. "Crawford & Zimmerman, Flint."

515 Rayon robe with yellow and browns. "Made expressly for West, Washington, DC."

516

517

516 Brown robe with white and green abstract design. No label.

517 Abstract robe with grey background.

518 Burgundy robe with abstract design. Label reads, "Robes by Stafford, Heyman-Fisher Co., Hamilton, Ohio."

519 Robe with grey background, yellow abstract design and black trim.

518

519

520

520 Rayon smoking jacket from the fifties. Grey with rust lining. The pattern has radios, tvs, and musical notes. No label.

521 Cotton Hawaiian pajama set with a red background. Label reads, "Nani of Hawaii."

521

522 Golf pajama, light blue. Made by "Textron."

523 Red pajamas "by Elaine Skiar" have ladies dancing the cancan surrounded by musical notes.

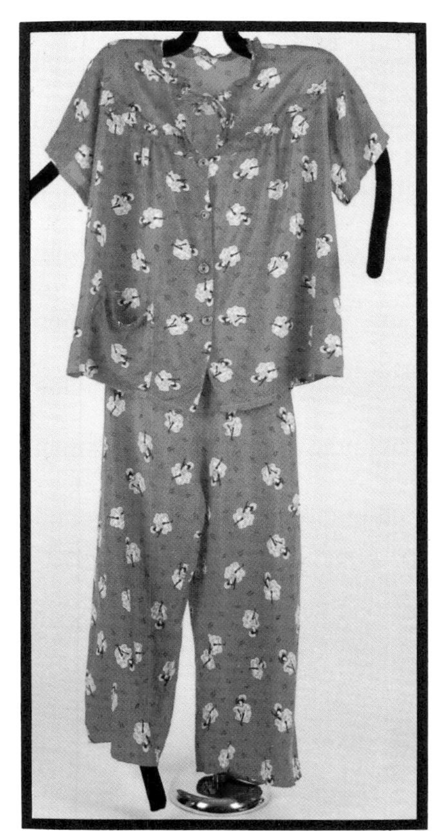

523

522

525

524

524 Green, black and white dress with leaf pattern. No label.

525 Decadent black robe, covered with lush, luxuriant feathers in bright pastels.

INSPIRED MOTIFS

COWBOYS, INDIANS & SOUTHWESTERN

1940s popular culture sought to escape the painful memories of the past war years. In order to do so, design adopted an escapist goal by centering on those things which had nothing to do with the war.

The southwestern motif was one such attempt at dissolving harsh memories of the war. The fascination with South America and Mexico was welcomed since these two countries had remained relatively untouched by the war. Southwestern and Native American scenes were adorned on textiles and fabrics of the era.

The Native American weavings provided the inspiration for a genre of earth-toned designs often based on geometric designs such as zigzags, diamonds and other angular shapes. These designs, because they were abstract and new to the popular culture, gained in intensity in the 1940s and 1950s.

526

526 Dobbs Rancher hatbox.

527 Great cowboy boots. 12" high, leather.

528 Cowboy scarf with square dancers, man and woman roping, fences and wagon wheels, yellow border. "Acetate, hand screen printed."

529 1950s yellow cowboy print skirt with saddle, cowboy boot, hat, first prize ribbon, and off-yellow background. Label reads, "Peerless Sportswear." Cotton.

531

533

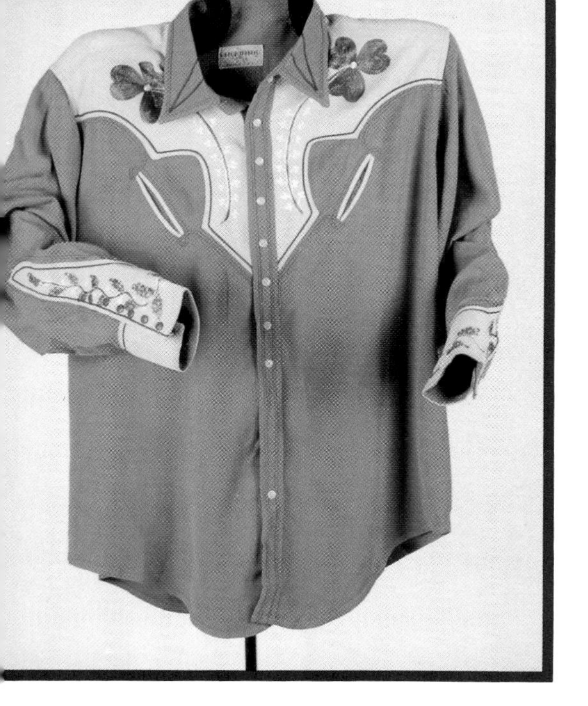

532

534

530 Indian boys with drums on abstract yellow lines that give the appearance of water with the blue.

531 Rodeo shirt in forest green and chartreuse yoke, and a red and green floral design, chartreuse fringe. No label.

532 Cowboy style with a coffee brown background and a chartreuse and yellow floral yoke. "S.A. Formann Co. Inc. Buffalo NY."

533 Black rodeo shirt with white fringe, pink and green flowers, and decorated with rhinestones. Label reads "S.A. Formann Co. Inc. Buffalo NY."

534 Cream colored shirt with gold and black sequined butterflies and black fringe. Label reads, "S.A. Formann Co. Inc., Buffalo, NY."

536

537

535 Two cowgirls in pink show off their stuff in these ceramics wall hangings.

536 Frosted cowboy glass, another common theme in the fifties, showing a lot of action.

537 Flat "Davy Crockett" shoulder bag.

538 Fabric with Mexican, Southwestern, squiggle and leaf pattern. Very Sante Fe, Southwestern looking.

539 Same fabric design in yellow and brown with black.

540

540 Hand painted back panel shirt, Southwestern motif with sombrero. "B.V.D. brand." No. 2 size.

541 Hawaiian shirt with palm trees and sombrero motif. Red gold, grey and black. Label reads, "Town Topic." XL.

542 Textile from the fifties with Mexican man with guitar and lady with tray on head.

542

54

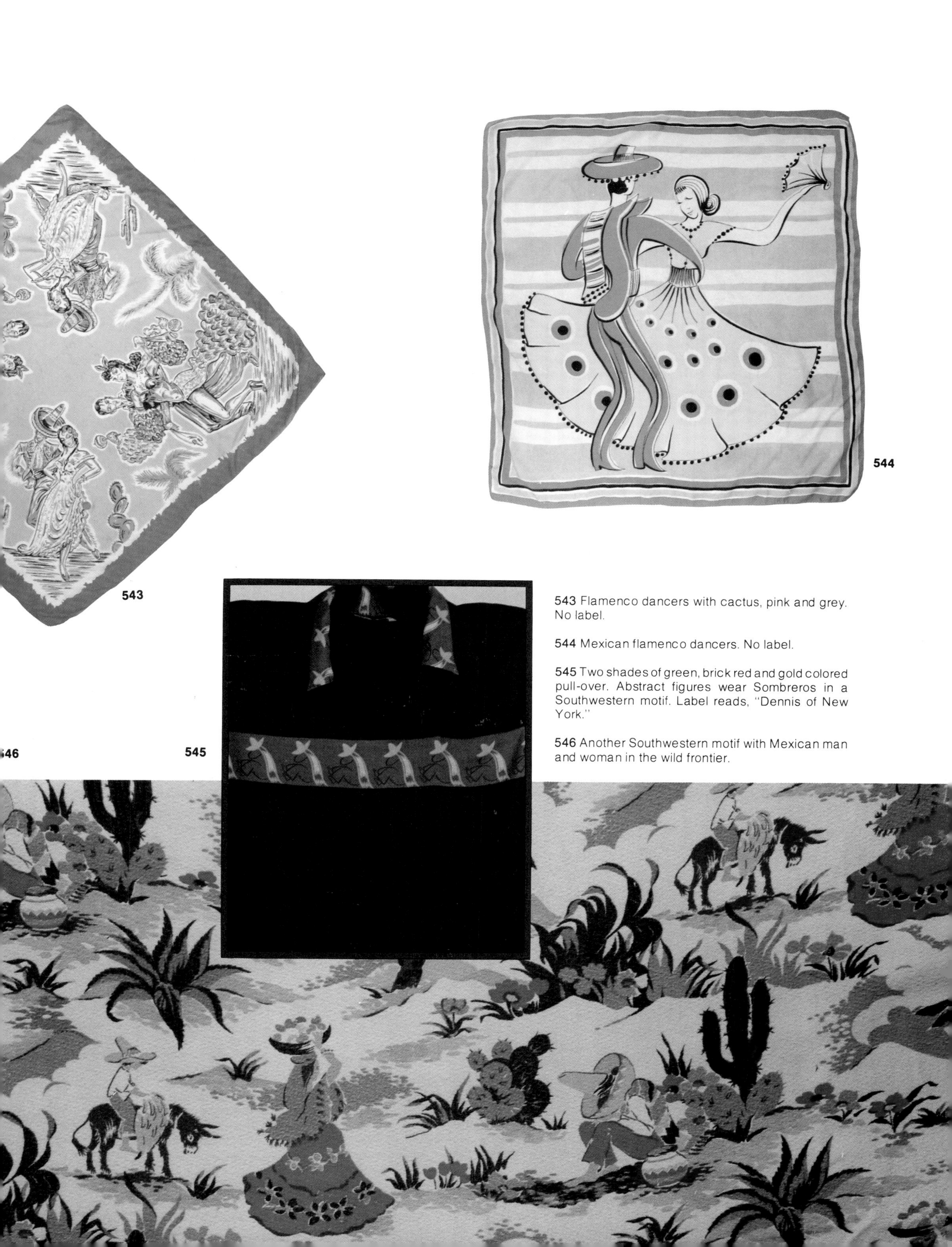
543

544

545

546

543 Flamenco dancers with cactus, pink and grey. No label.

544 Mexican flamenco dancers. No label.

545 Two shades of green, brick red and gold colored pull-over. Abstract figures wear Sombreros in a Southwestern motif. Label reads, "Dennis of New York."

546 Another Southwestern motif with Mexican man and woman in the wild frontier.

547

548

547 Black and white cowboy jacket with palamino appliqué on both sides. Label reads, "HbarC California Ranchwear."

548 Pink and black cowboy shirt with floral motif. "Hbar C California Ranchwear." Size M.

549 Perrywinkle blue and white cowboy style jacket with floral embroidery and black and white braiding. Snaps. "Mac Murray of California."

550 Avocado color, floral western shirt, heavy gabardine.

551 Cowboy style gabardine jacket. Label reads, "California Ranchwear."

551

549

550

552 Cowboy motif with red border and rope all around it. Abstract design with purple, chartreuse and orange background. No label.

553 Rayon square scarf with cowboy round up motif.

554 Small cowboy scarf which reads, "Gold claim, Wild West." No label.

555 Chartreuse rayon square scarf with the fringes. No label.

556 Small purple ascot or bandana. "The round up let 'er Buck." 17" x 16".

557 Cowboy scarf with the bucking bronco. No label. Red, yellow, white and grey with a guitar-playing cowboy.

558 Silk scarf with mexican jugs and the names of Mexican cities. No label. Silk.

559

560

559 Western scene tablecloth with white background.

560 Western design of a town on a piece of fabric.

561 "Pikes Peak or bust" written on the decorative covered wagons. The earthy tone background gives the appearance of the wild west so popular in the fifties.

562 Southwestern scene with man fishing.

563 Saloon and restaurant on red ground "shrunkatized." color-tested fabric.

564 Indian scene on a green background.

565 Bolt of fabric marked, "Puritan Vat Print" "Design copyright Lone Ranger."

566 Waverly pattern, called "Chuck Wagon." Different scenes on white are placed on the red background.

567 Western scene on a rayon and cotton blend, divided by rope pattern.

568 Fabric representing a Western landscape with earthy tones.

561

562

NO CREDIT

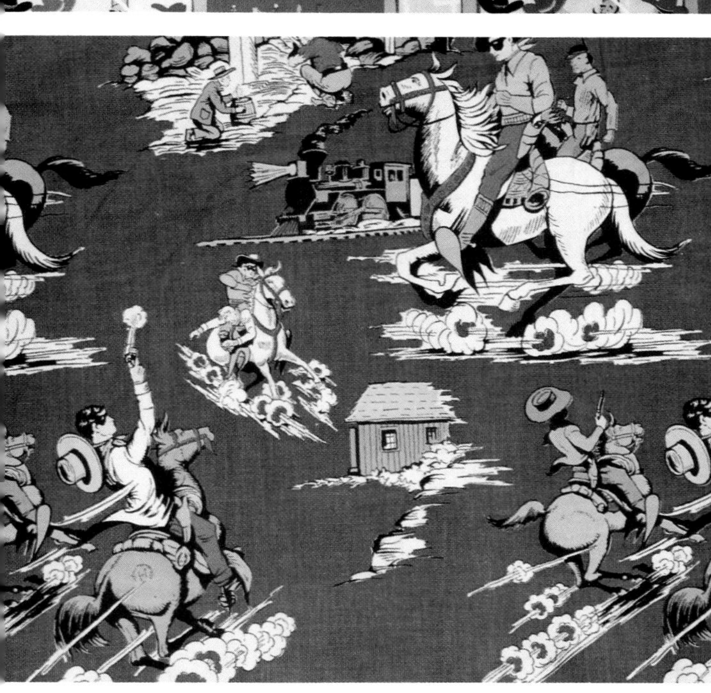

569 Interesting rayon cowboy style shirt with snaps. The shirt has a cowboy photoprint motif. Some people would call it a silkie or Hawaiian shirt because it is rayon. "Rockmount Ranchwear, Denver Colorado, Original."

570 Cowboy skirt with chartreuse background. Restaurant and bar scene with sequins sewn all over it. Advertises fried chicken and no credit. No label.

571

572

573

574

571 Pictorial cowboy shirt depicting a cactus, sun, and stagecoach in back. Label reads, "HbarC Ranchwear, NY LA." Dry clean only. Size L.

572 Forest green and pale green stage coach shirt. Label reads, "HbarC California." Size L.

573 Charcoal and beige saddle shirt. Label reads, "HbarC Ranchwear, NY, LA." Size M.

574 Black shirt with grey-blue yoke with playing cards. Label reads, "HbarC California Ranchwear." Size Large.

575

575 Black cowboy motif shirt. Raised painted dots to form cowboy boots, saddles, spurs. Label reads, "Western Wear by Beau Brummel."

576 Child's Hopalong Cassidy shirt in brown and hot pink stain yoke. Label reads, "The little champ of Hollywood, Made in California." Size 14.

577 Women's shirt with cowboy and calf being roped. Salmon color with black yoke. Label reads, "Connie Sportswear Denver."

578 Women's pale pink and brown cowboy shirt with roping horseback riders and cowboys on horseback with ropes. Label reads, "Western Maid Axler-Denver."

576

577

578

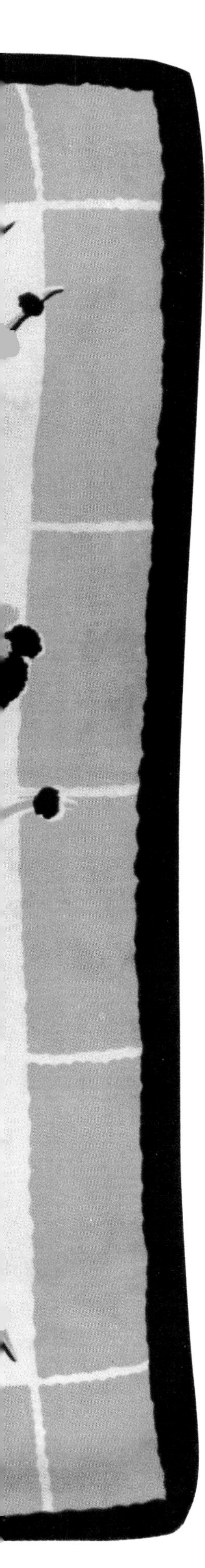

POODLES & PARISIENNE

Although France may have been placed "on hold" as the fashion leader of the world in the fifties, the returning service men brought home a renewed fascination with French culture and in the fifties it became a craze with the American population. Anything related to Paris was popular and designers of the day seized upon this. The French poodle, the Eiffel tower, beret and Bohemian artistic images became some of the most well-known motifs in the fifties.

Other common motifs were Parisienne scenes, as Paris gradually was rebuilt after the war, and people began to travel for pleasure again. Lautrecian café scenes and poodles were displayed delightfully in all sorts of fifties objects. In the 1957 film *Will Success Spoil Rock Hunter?* Jayne Mansfield wore outfits identical to those of her poodle, and they took baths together! José Ferrer played Lautrec in the film *Moulin Rouge* (1953).

The Paris Follies took place in 1956 and the craze took off in full force. Anything Parisienne was considered gay and uplifting. From women's scarves to their poodle skirts, the mood reflected the sentiment of "gay Paree" from the standpoint of America. Although many never traveled to the country, many Americans in the fifties got a popular taste for the Parisienne culture.

579 Poodle cookie jar by "Sierra Vista Ceramics. Pasadena, Calif."

580 Papier maché poodle. 22.5" high.

581 Poodles stand alert (if sometimes upside-down) on this Fifties scarf.

581

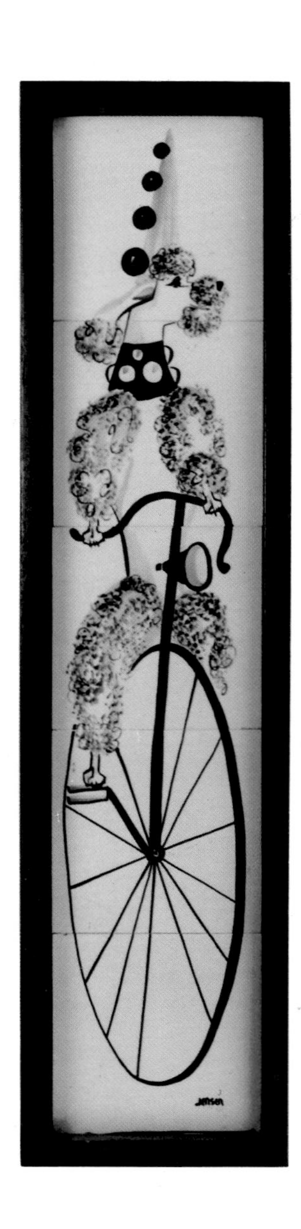

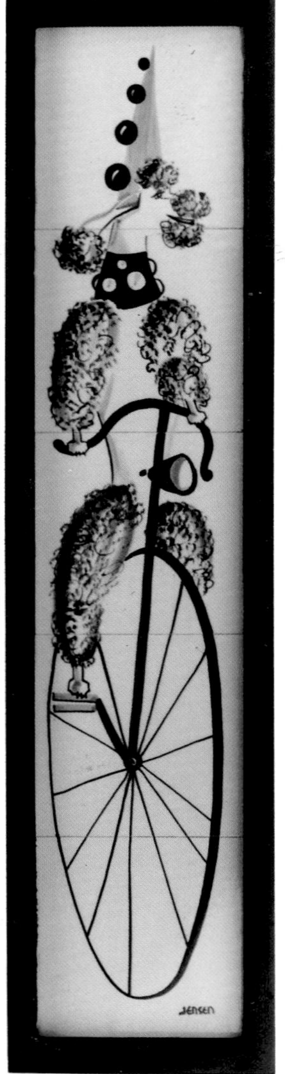

582

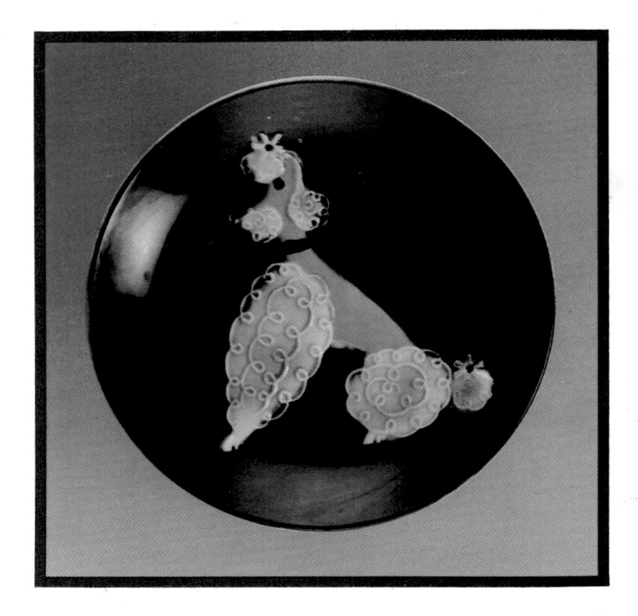

583

584

582 Another set of tiles by Jensen of poodles, constructed of five, six inch tiles. The poodles must be from the circus considering their bicycles and yellow and pink hats.

583 Poodle dish with decorative poodle.

584 As the television became a common household object, they began to be thought of as yet another piece of furniture and ornaments were manufactured to decorate them. This pink and black TV lamp, with bulbs hidden in the back, is one such ornament. Possibly marked, Lane & Co. 16.5" x 13".

585

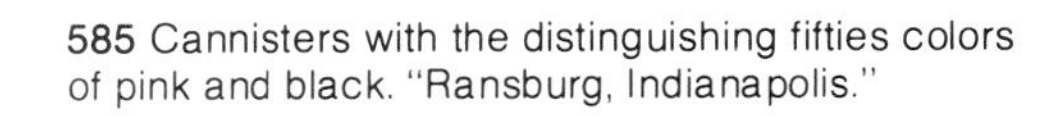

585 Cannisters with the distinguishing fifties colors of pink and black. "Ransburg, Indianapolis."

586 This television-top poodle lamp carries a common fifties motif as well as a fifties purpose. 11" x 10".

586

587

587 Bathing poodle adorns a metal wastebasket. 13" x 9" x 8".

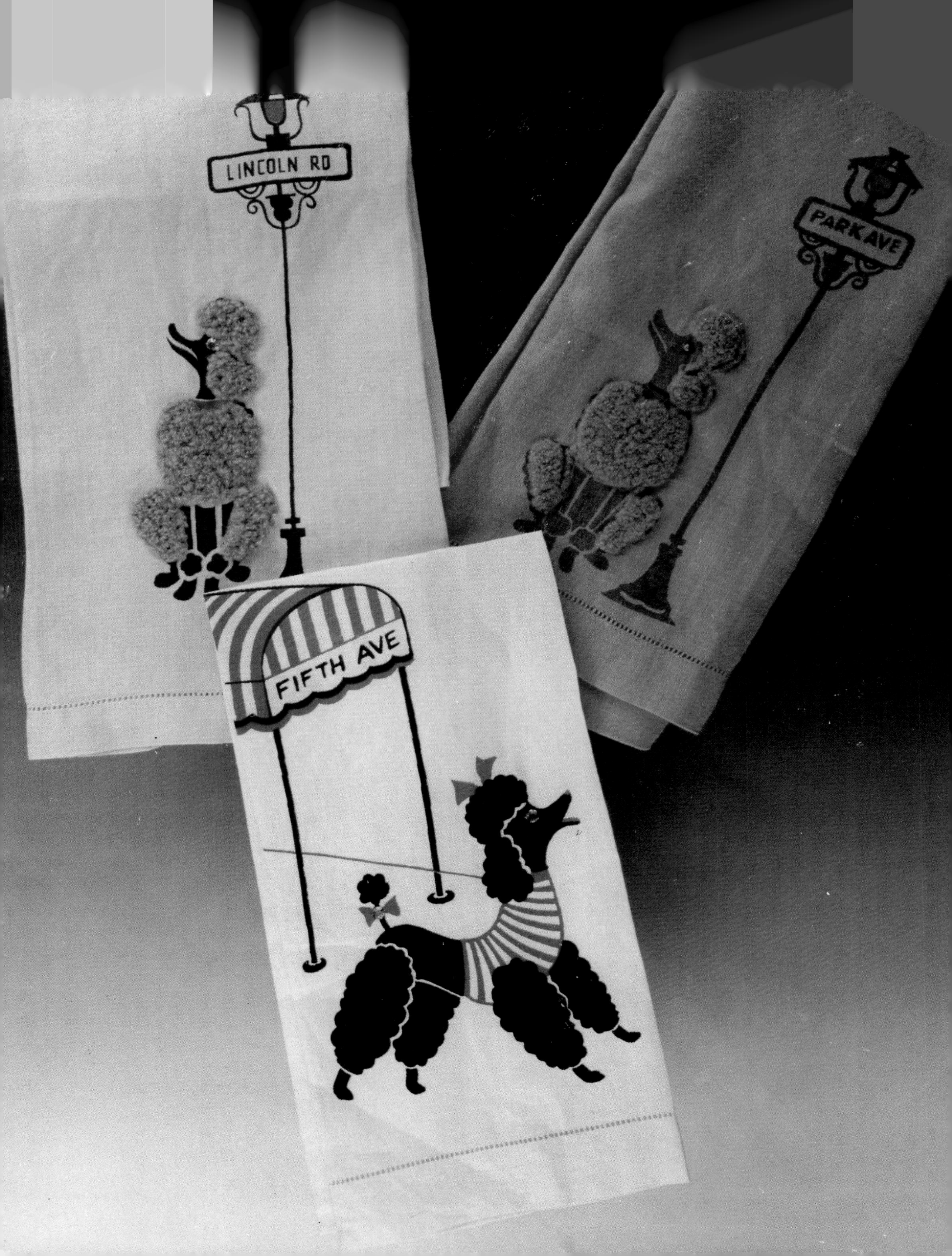
LINCOLN RD
PARK AVE
FIFTH AVE

589

590

591

588 Three hand towels with poodles on famous streets, "Park Ave," "Fifth Ave" and "Lincoln Rd."

589 Cybis poodles. Ceramic. Small: 10" high. Larger: 15" high.

590 An appropriate pink cover for *The Poodle, Its Origin History & Varieties*. By T.H. Tracy. Published by The Poodle Speciallty Shop, 1950.

591 Pink poodles with rhinestone bellybuttons. Taller: 12.5", Zali design, Redwood California. On green stand: 11" x 8" x 6", signed Jane Callender.

592 Cigarette dish and ashtray with some snazzy poodles, marked "Cloisenamel."

593 One of Sascha Brostoff's favorite subjects, the poodle on vases and ashtrays. Signed, "Sascha B."

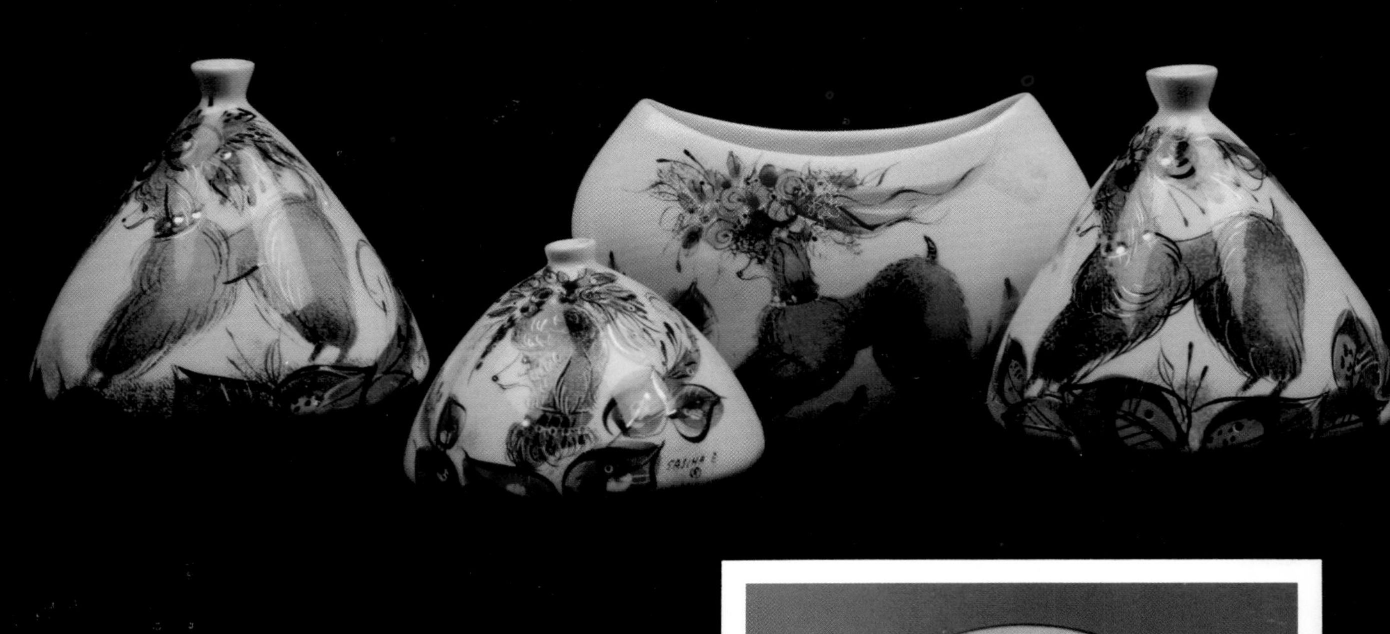

592

594 Wire wall hangings have a man and woman reading newspapers at the Café De La Paix. A poodle faces the woman reading *Vogue.*

595 Dish with poodle inserting a hat pin while glancing in the mirror. Signed, "Lelah."

596 Poodle made of shells and beads sitting on velvet. 12.5" x 10.5".

594

595

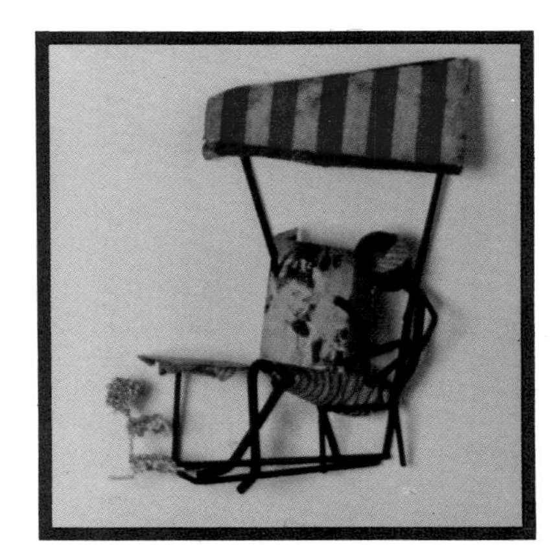

596

597

597 "April in Paris" poodle tray. By "Nashco Products, New York." Signed by the artist, Clement.

598 Poodle tray, metal. Two poodles have a drink at a porch table.

598

599 Mr. and Mrs. poodle at the park bench reading *Le Figaro* while the younger poodles play. "The romance of fe fe and pepe. Kentley Corporation, Grand Rapids, MI."

599

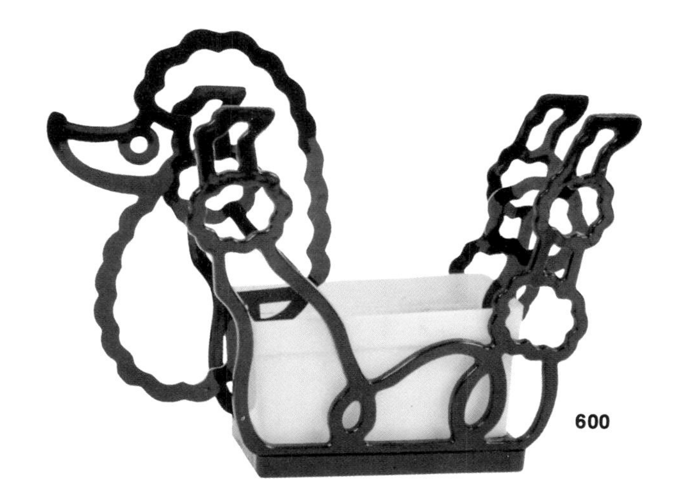

600 Plastic planter in the shape of a poodle.

601 Pink vinyl poodle lunch box with a matching thermos. Signed, "Aladdin Industries Inc. Nashville Tenn."

602 Poodles with umbrellas on an apron, orange and yellow with black trim.

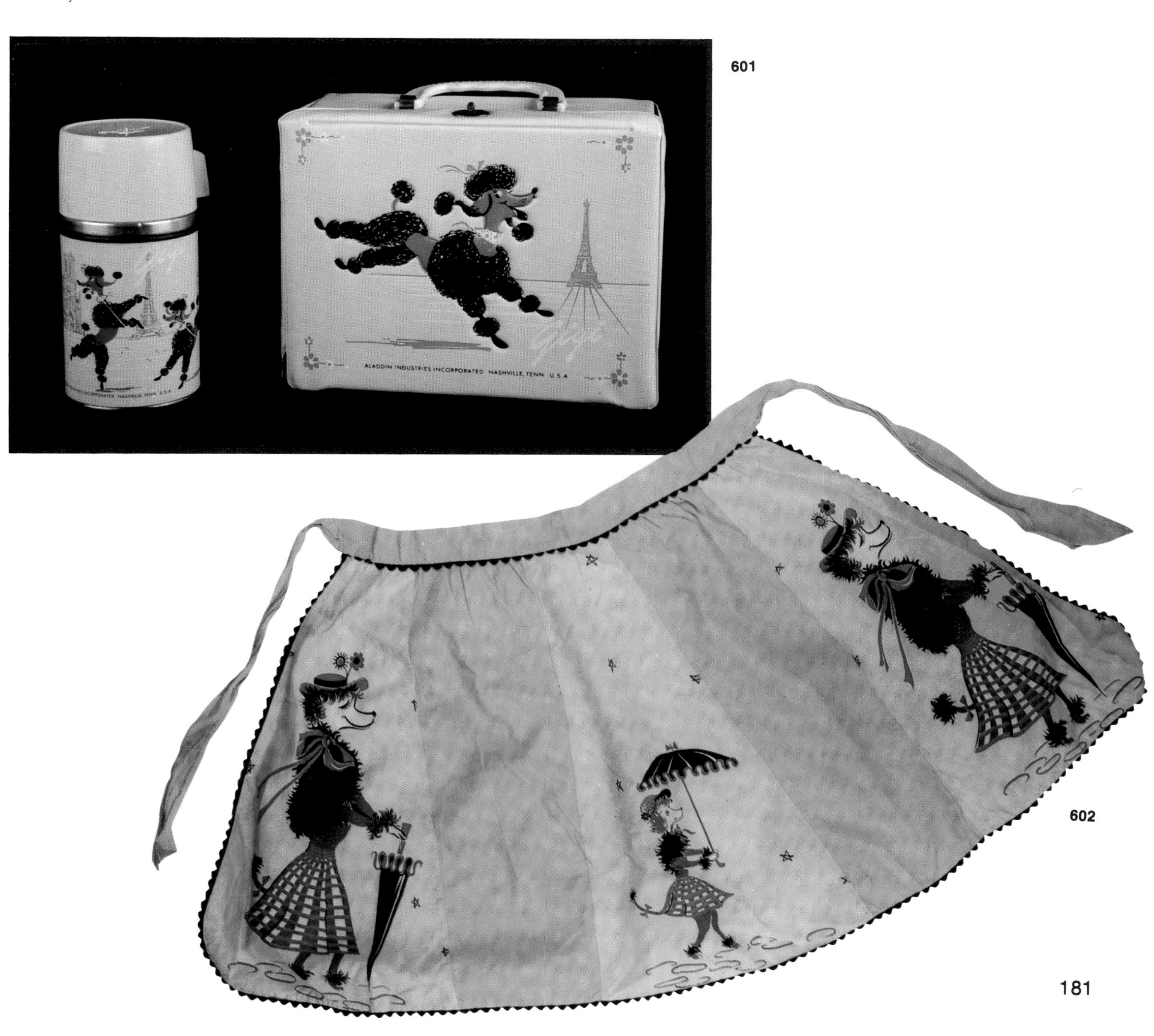

603 Ooh la la poodle bag, poodle with umbrella vinyl and bamboo handle. Marked, "Magid."

604 Parasol with poodle head.

605 Risqué! Boxer shorts with inch measure and words, "wanna play with my poodle."

603

604

605

606 Red felt bag with grey poodle. No label.

606

607

607 MiMi the poodle jumps across this vinyl bag. No label.

608

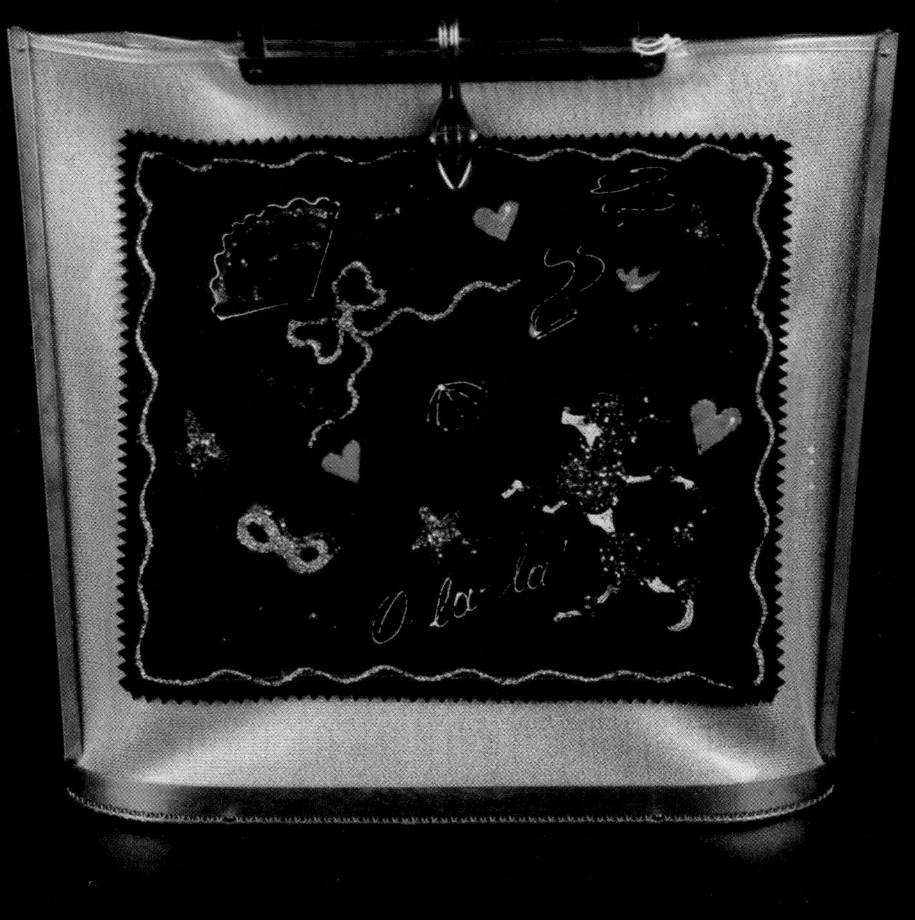

609

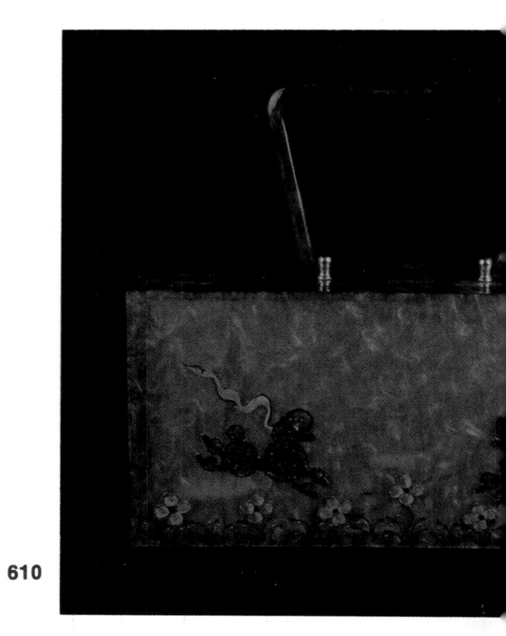

610

611

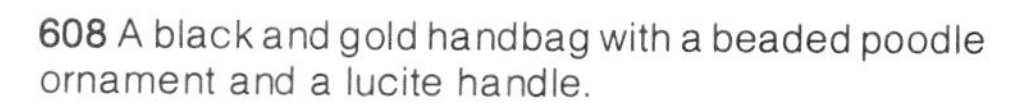

608 A black and gold handbag with a beaded poodle ornament and a lucite handle.

609 Poodle bag, "o-la-laa." Gold and black.

612

610 Bakelite poodle bag by Wilardy, New York.

611 Mother-of-pearl plastic bag with a decorative poodle on the front. No label.

612 Black and gold poodle bag with a coin collar, trimmed in metal. No label.

613 Poodle bag, "take me places" with gold metallic. Label reads, "Claire Fashion."

614 Black and gold poodle bag, lucite top and lucite covered with black felt.

615 Pink and black poodle bag with silver, glittered, woven plastic sides. No label.

613

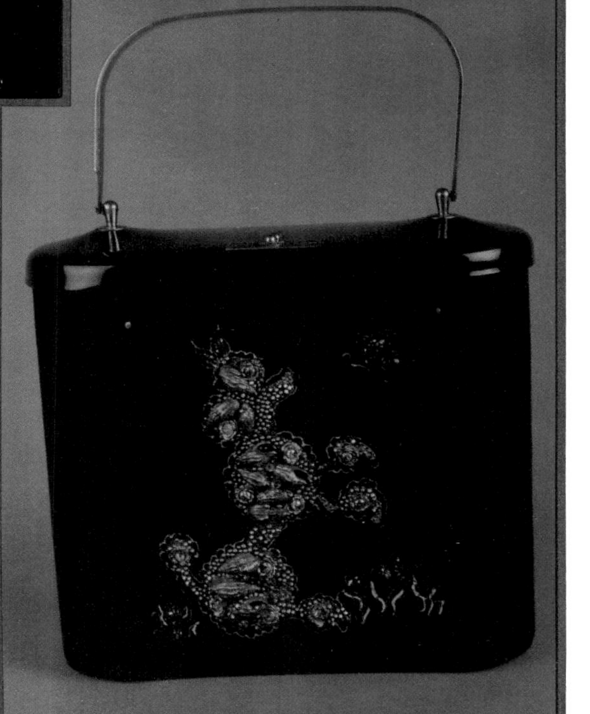

614

615

616 Black felt poodle bag with tapestry. No label.

617 Poodle bag with squiggles and a pink and white poodle. No label.

618 Black velvet poodle bag with big red ribbon. Marked, "Jolles Original."

619 Grey and white poodle on fabric bag with bell and green ribbon in hair. Label reads, "Jolles Original."

616

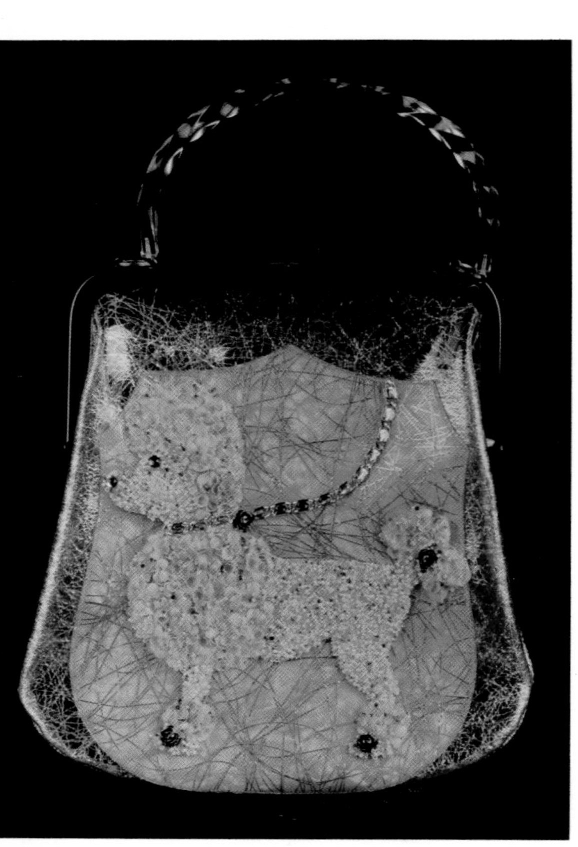

617

619

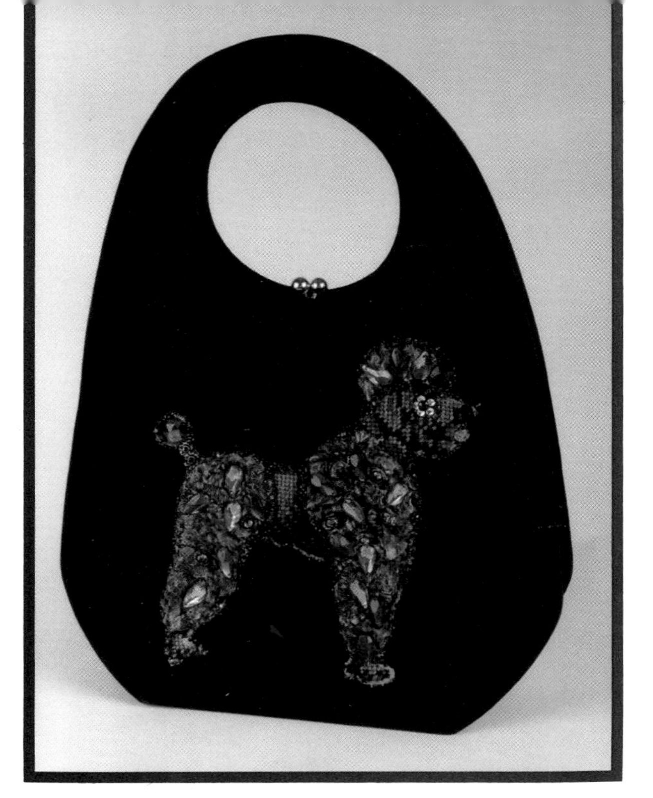

620

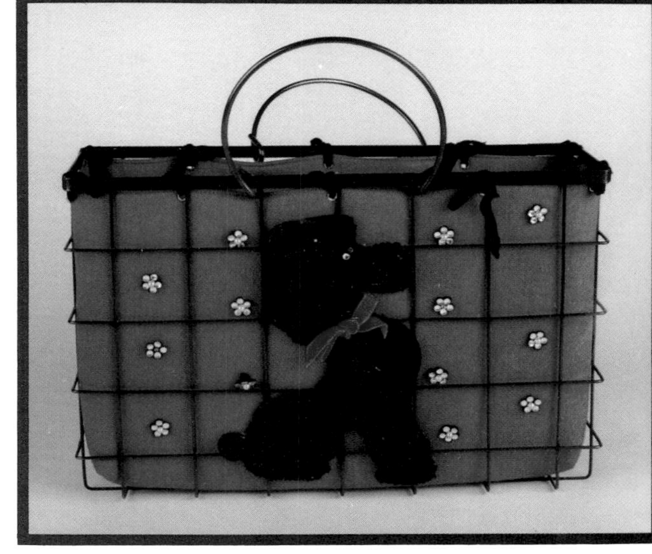

621

622

618

620 Black velvet poodle bag with poodle decorated with cut stones. No label.

621 Poodle wire basket. A blue fabric with rhinestones and a black poodle make this truely a fifties original. Label reads, "Jolles Original."

622 Felt poodle bag embellished with decorative poodle. Label reads, "La France."

623 Velvet poodle bag. No label.

623

624 Vinyl poodle bag.

624

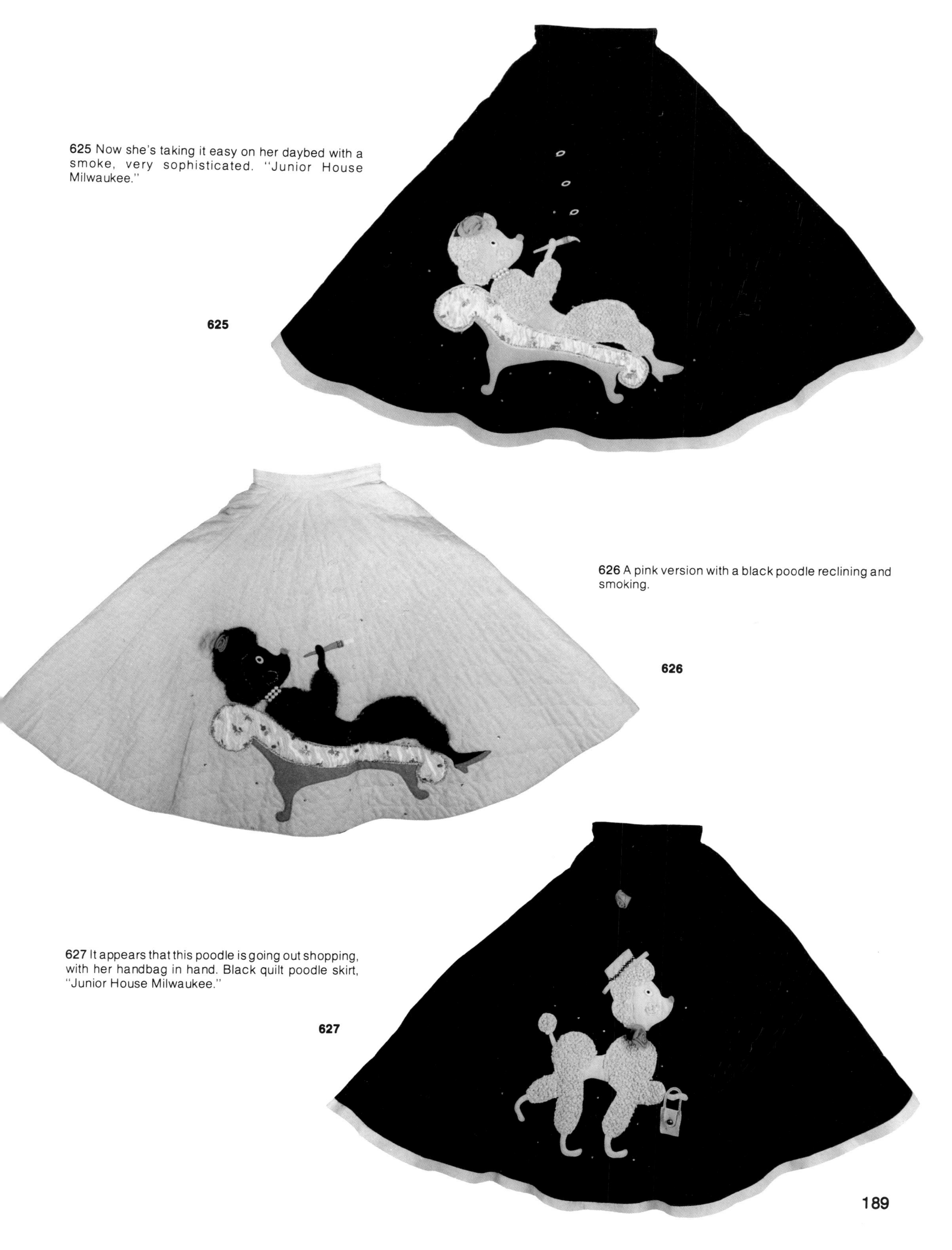

625 Now she's taking it easy on her daybed with a smoke, very sophisticated. "Junior House Milwaukee."

625

626 A pink version with a black poodle reclining and smoking.

626

627 It appears that this poodle is going out shopping, with her handbag in hand. Black quilt poodle skirt, "Junior House Milwaukee."

627

628

628 "Garay," mother and three baby poodles on an orange beaded leash.

629 Souré bag with pink glittered poodle on front. Vinyl.

630 Red velvet handbag with just a suggestion of a heart-shape, featuring an embroidered poodle with crocheted black accenting.

629

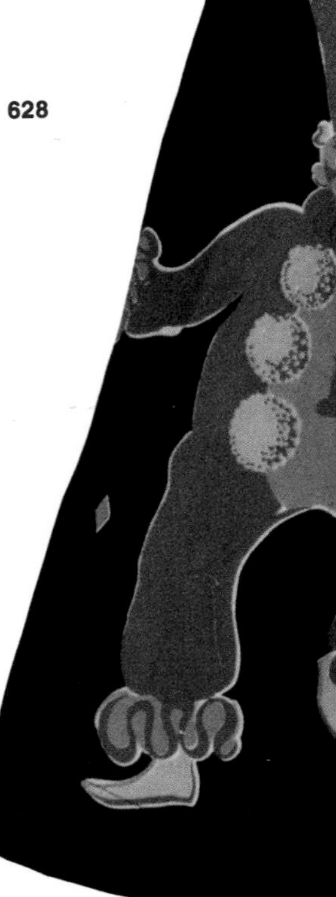

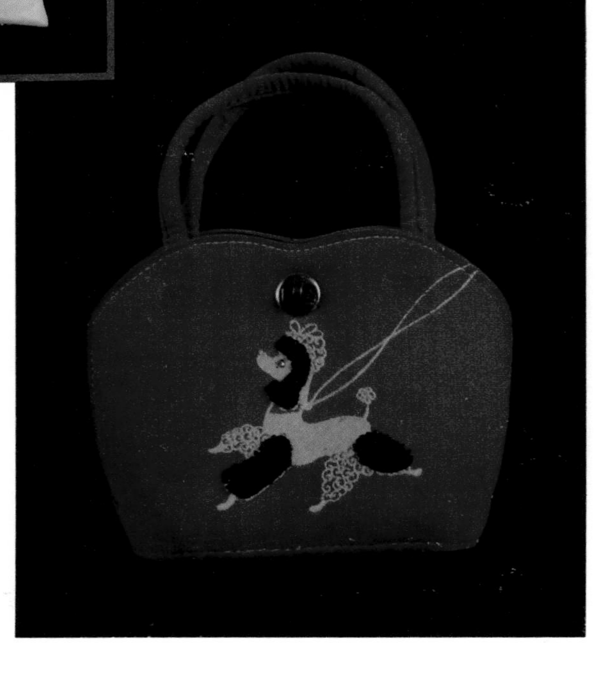

630

631 1950s circle poodle skirt with clowns on front and harlequin diamonds on a black background.

632 Talented poodles decorate this bag. "You can't teach an old dog new tricks." No label.

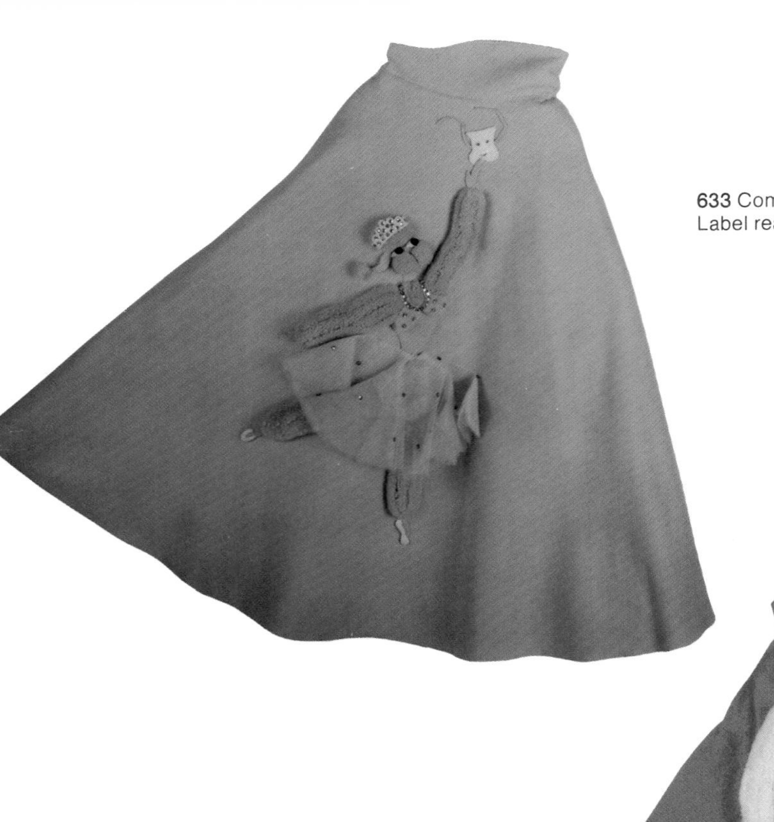

633 Comical poodle ballerina embellishes this skirt. Label reads, "Kinneloa of California, Pasadena, 8."

634 Hot pink gabardine poodle skirt. The poodle has her own skirt. Label reads, "Kinneloa of California, Pasadena, 8."

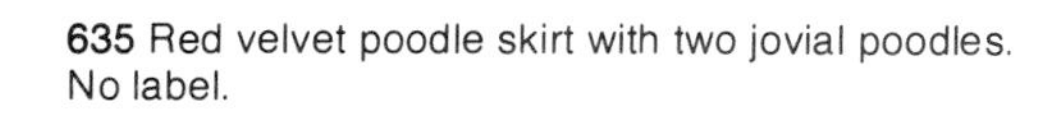

635 Red velvet poodle skirt with two jovial poodles. No label.

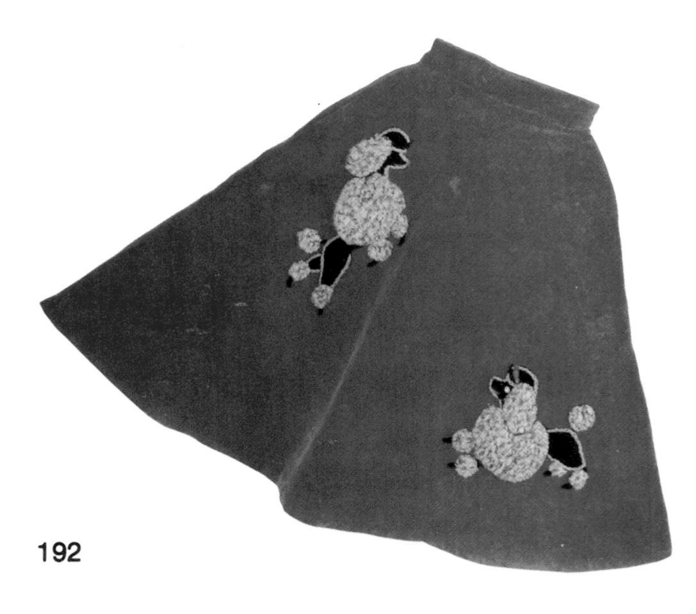

636 White cotton skirt with poodles in carriages with their mothers and umbrellas.

638 Straw and vinyl poodle bag with the Eiffel Tower. The fifties were enthralled by Gay Paris. Label reads, "Tropic, Miami Florida."

637

637 Very sophisticated black and white poodle with sequins and the eiffel tower on a handbag.

638

640

640 Poodle and butterfly bag. No label.

639

639 Poodle bag, black and white poodles straw and velvet. "An Original of Midis of Miami Handcrafts in Miami Florida."

64

643

641 Lavendar swing coat with a cut velvet black poodle with gold balls on its collar and a red mouth and eye. Made of linen, no label.

642 Navy, cashmere jacket with Parisienne motifs. Long Beach, Calif. and New York.

643 Another poodle hoop dress with poodles in lavendar ribbons. Label reads, "Serbin of Florida."

644 Corduroy poodle skirt with lavendar poodles, no label.

645 Whimsical cotton dress with orange, yellow and green balloons attached to a poodles tail. No label.

646 Linen pink and black dress marked, "Styled by Sacson." The print has poodles jumping through hoops.

644

646

645

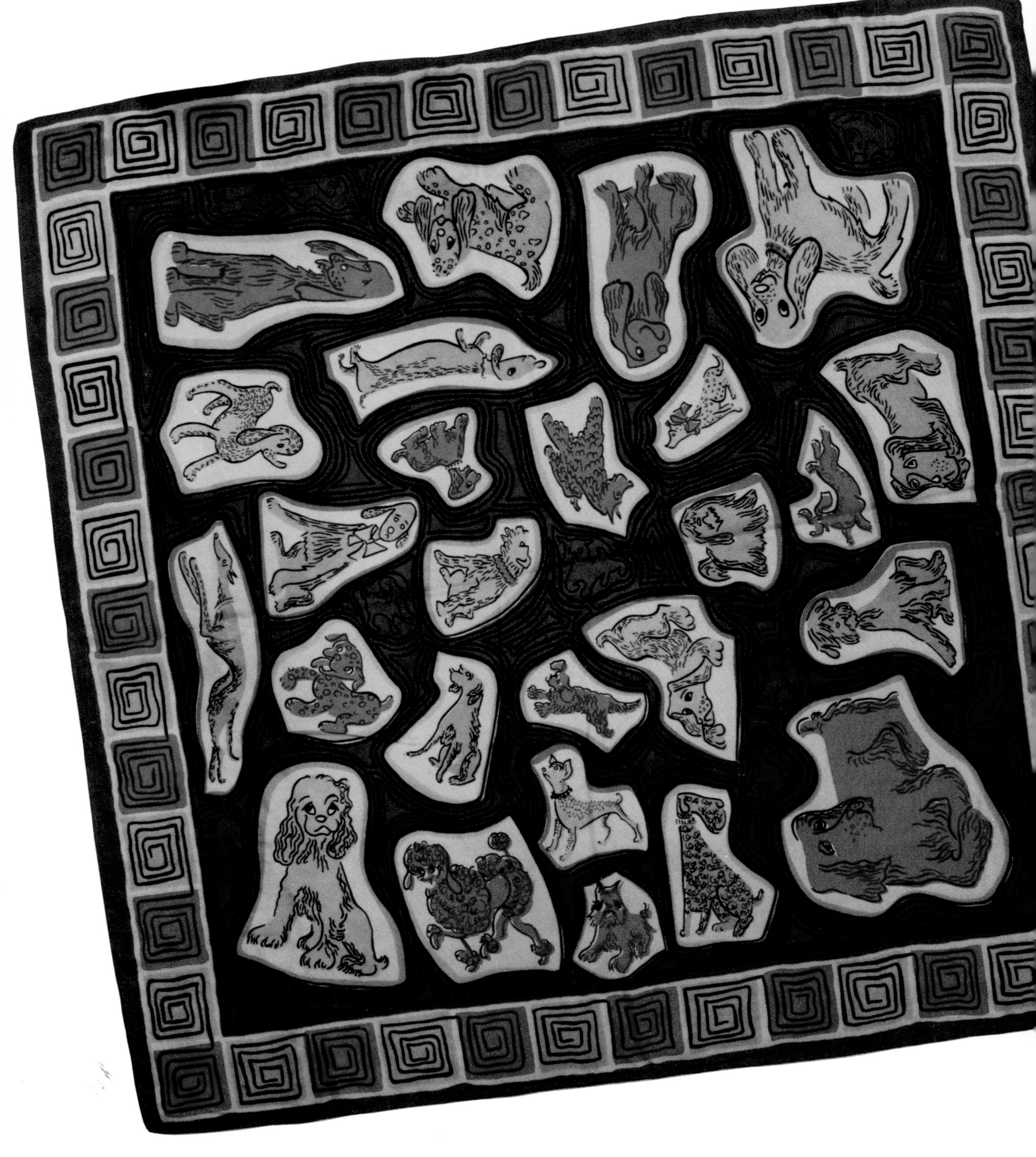

647 Poodle scarf with abstract dogs. Chartreuse, blue, coral black, white, and grey. Label reads, "Glentex, all silk."

648 Poodle scarf with dogs centered around a tree. "Glentex All Silk." Signed by Tammi S. Keefe.

649 Pink face poodle scarf. "A scarf by Kimbal, water repellent." The poodle looks at bread tied to a string.

650 The fifties were enthralled with everything French, including this policeman, who is treating two poodles to some delightful tidbit.

651 Scarf in aqua marked, "Created by Kimbal" with navy poodle with red ribbons.

652 Pastel scarf giving the appearance of clippings and headlines reading, "Jean de Botton Fou Fou discovers America."

653 Poodle scarf. Signed, "Tammi S Keefe." Silk. All the names of the poodles emanate from the center.

649

650

651

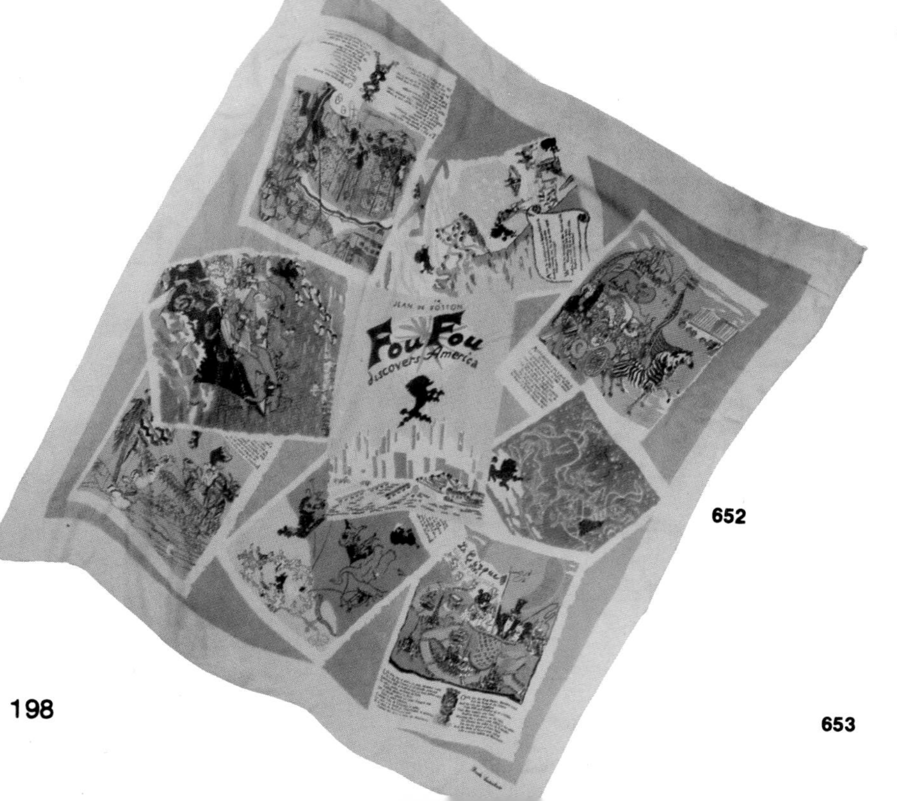

652

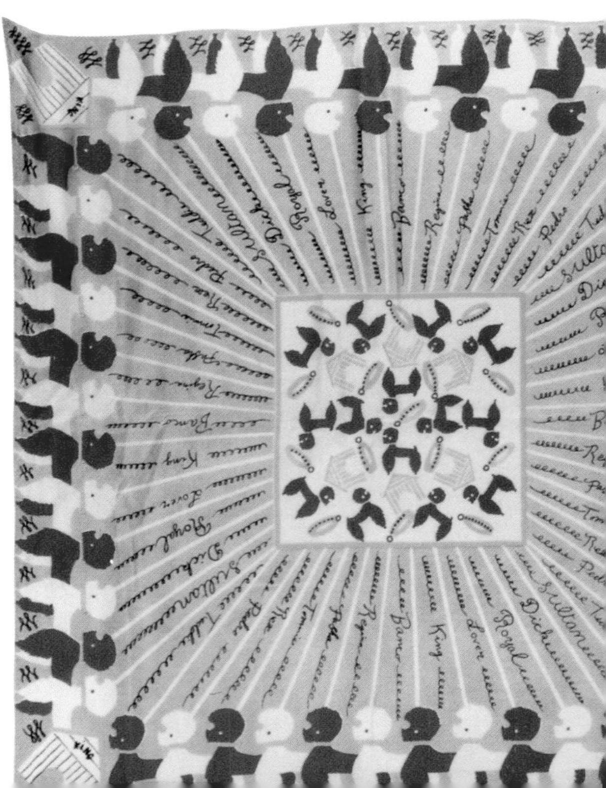

653

654 Light blue scarf with "oodles of poodles."

655 One-sided scarf with green polka dots on white background and navy poodles.

656 Scarf with a poodle dressed in red ribbons to match the red border.

657 Nifty fifties poodle scarf with lamp posts. Rayon.

658 Green and white checkered scarf with white and black poodles. Label reads, "Rayon and silk, chief value silk, hand rolled."

655

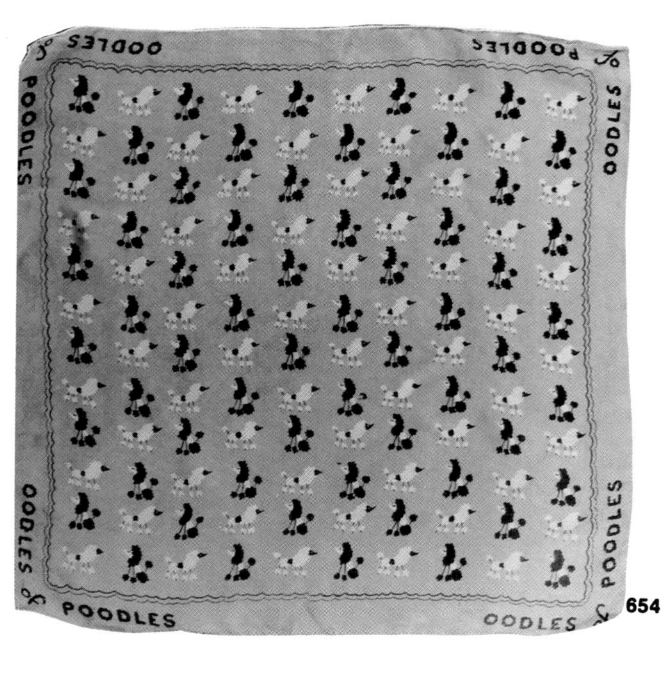

654

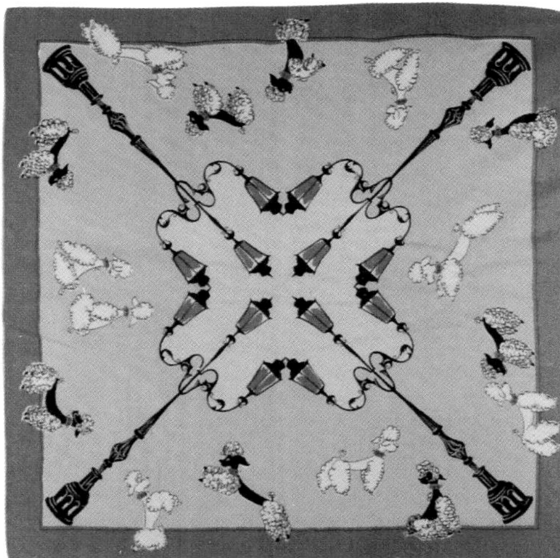

657

656

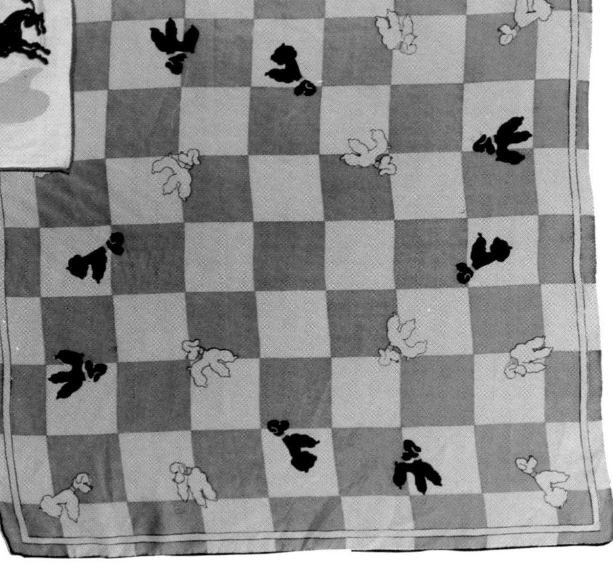

658

659

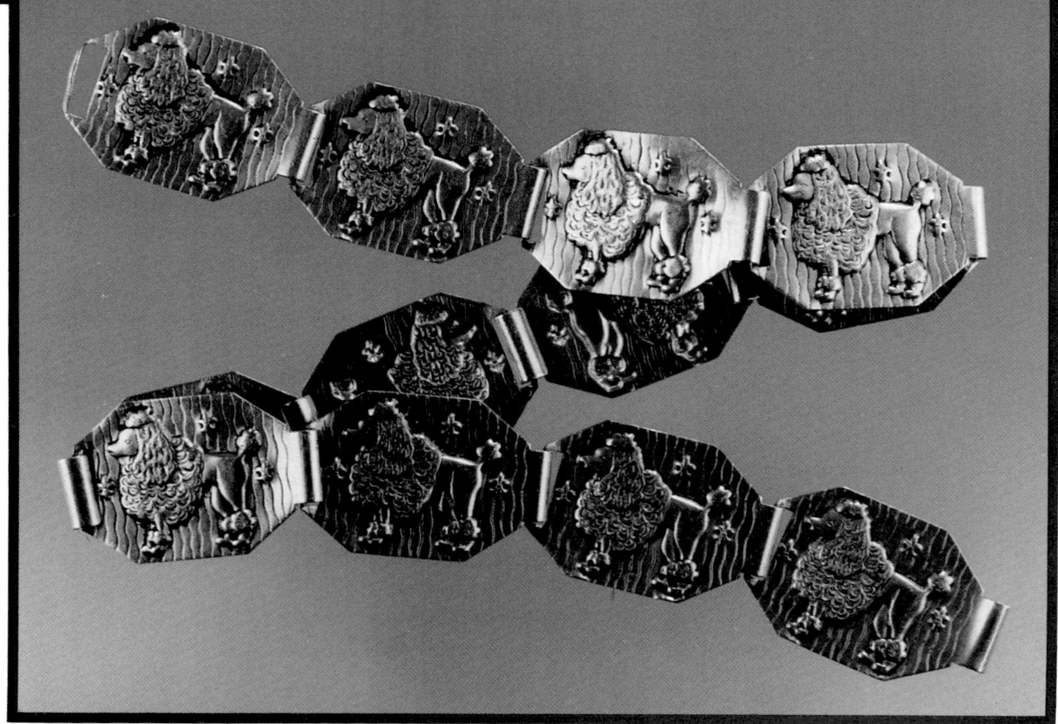

660

661

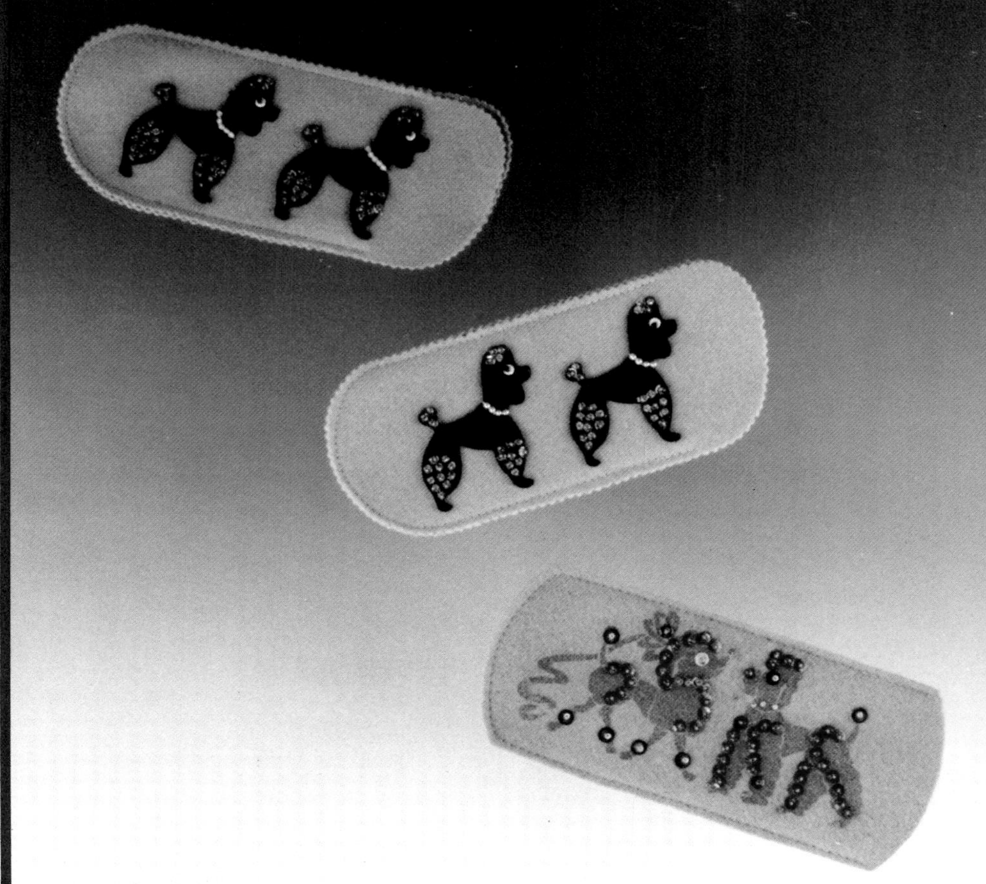

662

659 Delightful poodle compacts

660 They just could not get enough poodles. They were even imprinted on belts!

661 Poodle jewelry: small poodle with black and red ribbon, sterling; grey pearl poodle, marked Schreiner, New York; poodle with earrings, marked Schreiner, New York; red poodle, marked Kramer.

662 Ornamented poodle eyeglass cases.

HARLEQUINS

The harlequin figure often connotes that which is comic and whimsical in the theatre. That probably explains its popularity during the 1950s when the world was emerging from the war and turning a new face, one which could laugh and enjoy life, for once.

The harlequin diamond pattern became a common motif in many types of fifties objects, from Harlequin paintings and tiles, to harlequin sculpture, and harlequin designs in textiles. The harlequin pattern is also called the diamond, or argyle pattern.

663 Harlequin scarf in a more abstract form. No label.

664 A wonderful black, lavendar and white reversible jacket with harlequin diamond pattern. A real rock'n roll jacket. Reverse is solid lavendar. This diamond pattern has been called argyle, diamond pattern, and harlequin.

664

665 Harlequin musicians with their mandolins; one seems to be taking a break, while the other prepares to begin a new tune! Marked "#7053." Relief marked "R. F. Harnett by Metalcraft Corp."

666 Enamel harlequin of pink, black and gold by Sascha Brostoff. 15.5" x 8".

665

666

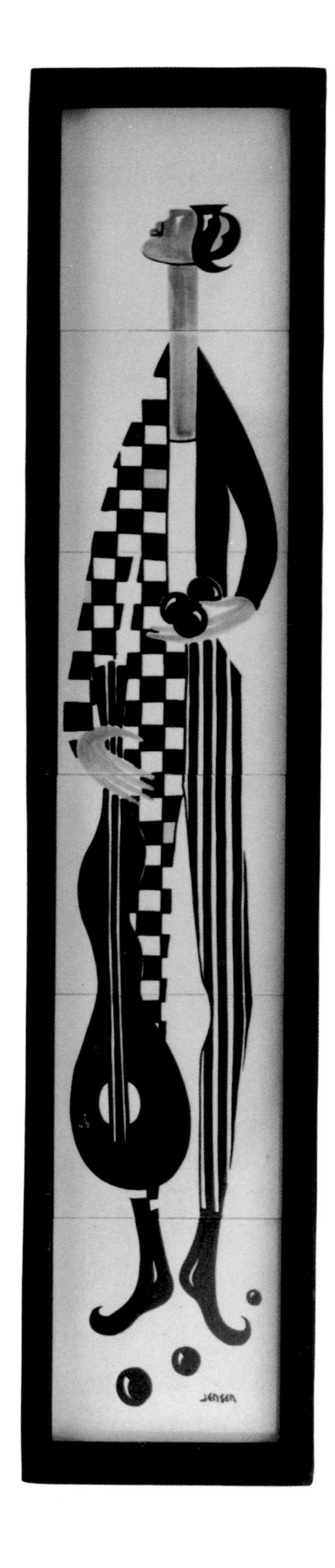

668

667

667 On either side, a harlequin wall hanging by the artist Jensen. Six inch square tiles and wooden frame. Black and white.

668 In the center, a painting of a harlequin on canvas board. Unsigned. 4.75" x 11.5".

669 Glazed ceramic with a musical theme.

670 Glass wall hangings of harlequins by the famous glassmakers from the fifties, Frances & Michael Higgins.

669

670

671 Scarf with men and women in harlequin diamonds dancing. Silk. No label.

672 Harlequin and ballerina on tight rope, and flower. Label reads, "Glentex Reg. US Pat Off, all silk."

671

672

673 Harlequin statue figure. Bellaire Porcelain. 28" high.

674 Harlequin painting by Meek. 11.5" x 15.5".

675 Bellaire candelabras with harlequins. One is marked, "Marc Bellaire Mardi Gras." 10.5" x 15".

673

674

675

676

677

678

676 Rayon fabric with a colorful harlequin design, no Label.

677 Polished cotton fabric in a harlequin pattern.

678 The all-time fifties favorite, pink and black diamond pattern.

679 Weinberg lamp, a well-known sculptor displaying two abstract people molded together as they play the guitar and violin. 27.5" high.

680 Harlequin fabric with harlequins playing guitar against a diamond background. Pure linen by Prints Charming.

681 Harlequin tin tray with abstract design in the background.

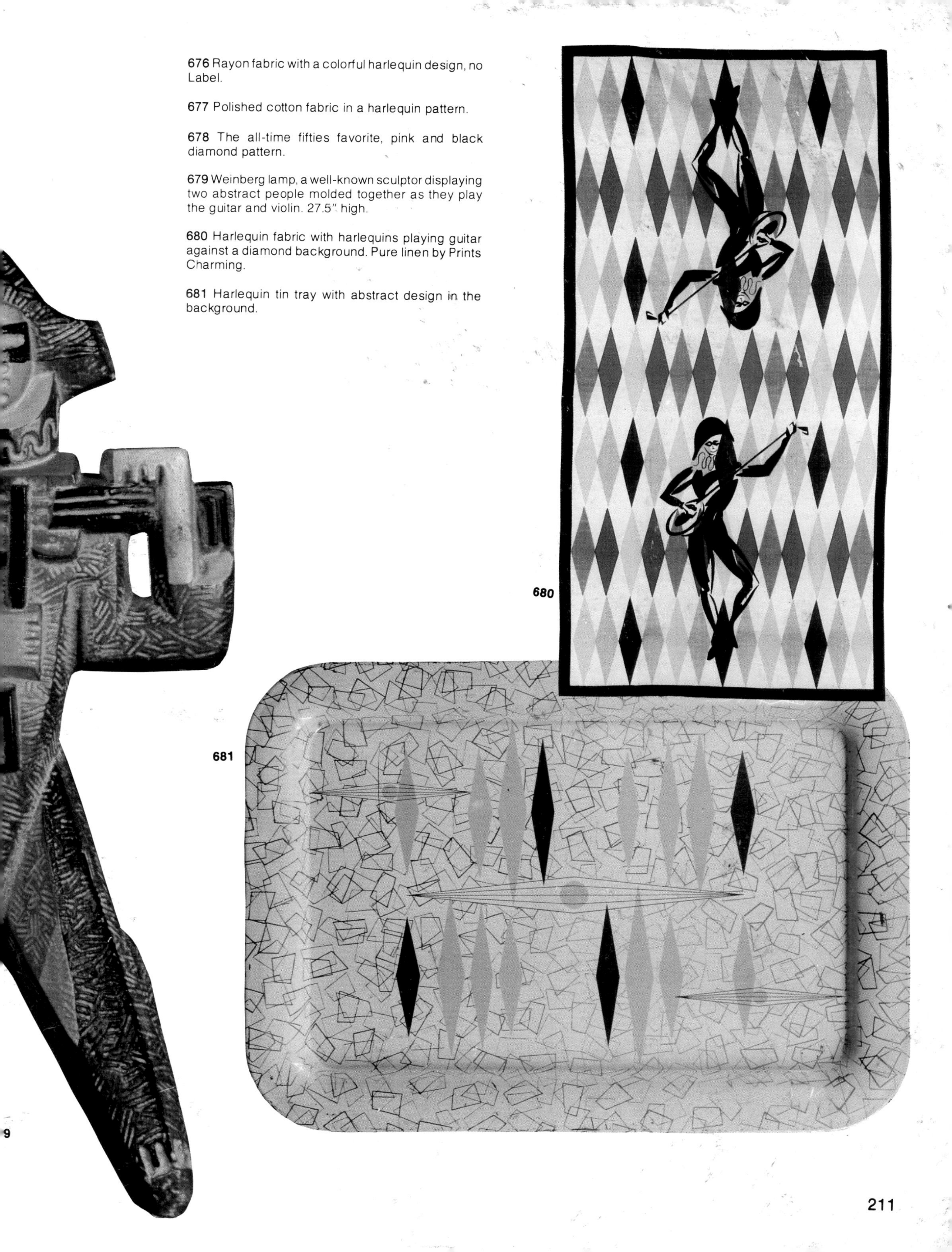

680

681

9

682 Harlequin, diamond pattern in navy, light blue and white. No label.

683 Rare white, orange, and grey diamond, argyle or harlequin jacket. Reversible to navy.

684 Comical handkerchief by Tom Lamb shows a duck going to school with a frog as the teacher.

685 "Pattern Zoo Train" by Rambler House. Train and track displayed.

FOR KIDS

686

Fabrics with popular cartoon characters, circus and zoo scenes were chosen for the childrens' room.

688

686 Fabric with the Alice in Wonderland print.

687 Fabric with a wonderful circus scene in bright colors.

688 Circus prints were popular for the children's room. No label.

689 The famous Blondie cartoon presented on a fabric. "Blondie, copyright by King Features, A Town and Country Vat Print."

690 Disneyland fabric with the Walt Disney characters.

691 Very artistic pattern on this fabric, possibly of Noah's ark.

692 Zoo animals appear behind cages on a polished cotton.

693 Fabric for the children's room with camping scenes. No label.

694 Cotton fabric with a zoo design. No label.

689

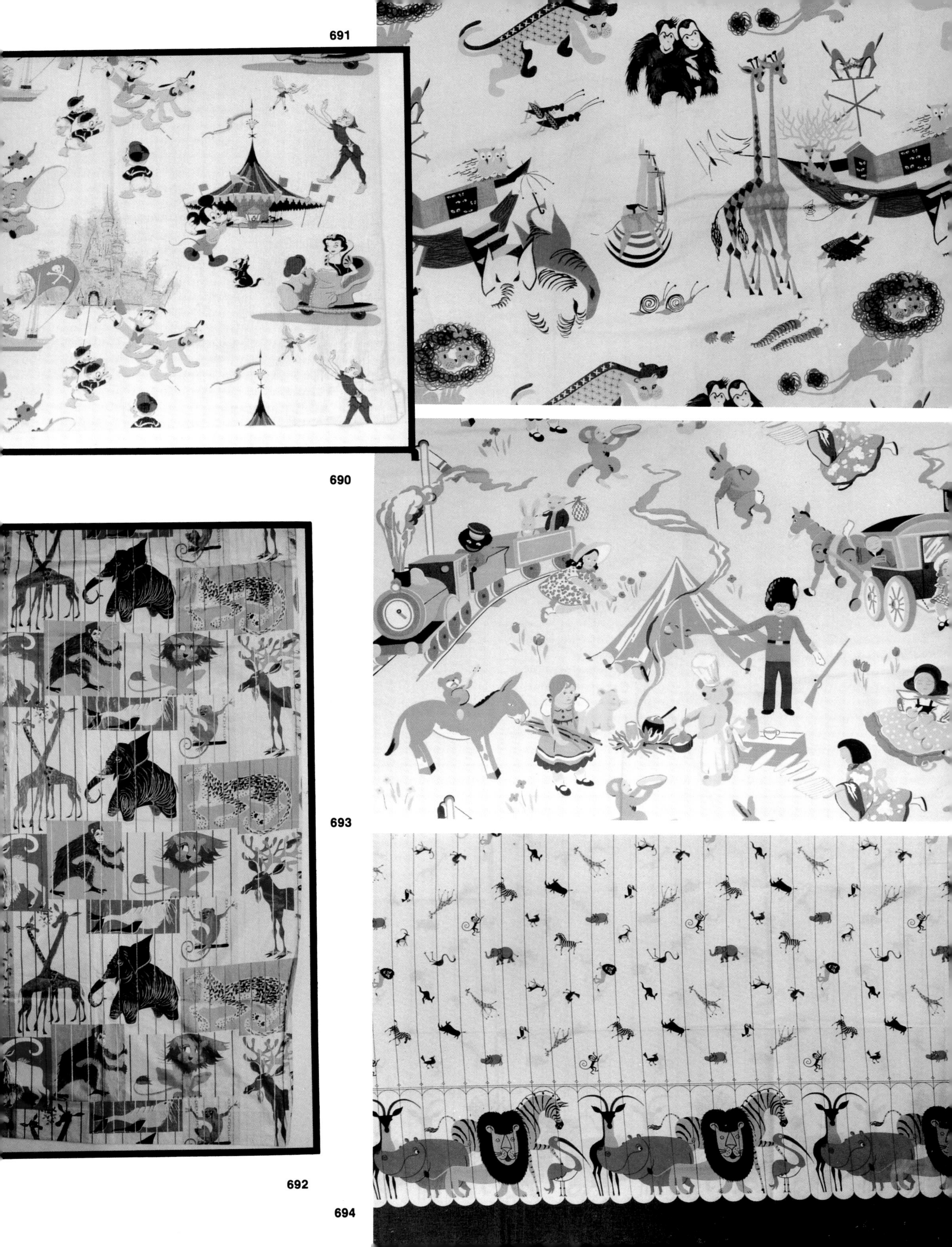
691
690
693
692
694

695 Davy Crockett shirt for child, pink or salmon colored with tan fringe on sleeves.

696 Adorable Hawaiian shirt for a child. "Kamehameha, made and styled in Hawaii."

697 Two-piece child's skirt and blouse, Dale Evans design.

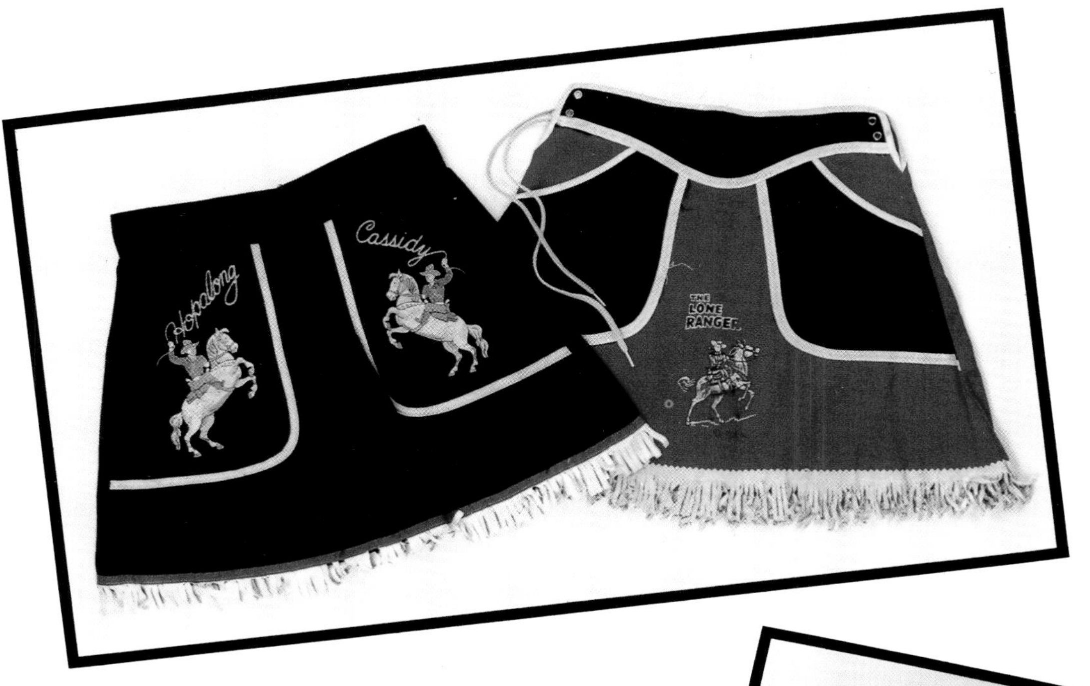

698 Lone Ranger child's skirt in red and black with fringe. Hopalong Cassidy child's skirt, all black.

699 Child's Hawaiian shirt with circus theme.

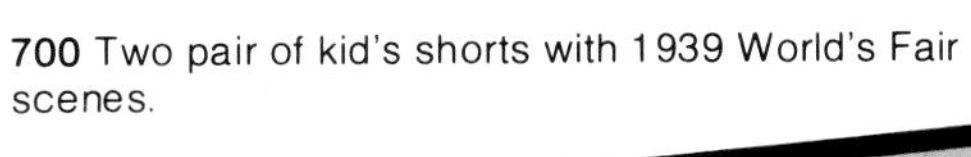

700 Two pair of kid's shorts with 1939 World's Fair scenes.

CONCLUSION ON COLLECTING

Collecting on a serious level is a truly fascinating endeavor. One of its many rewards includes invitations into the homes and closets of other serious collectors for what is often referred to as a "show and tell."

Collecting brings you into contact with others who are as driven as you are. They come from every conceivable walk of life, from the scientist to the movie star; the construction worker to the athlete. Steinberg says she has two different groups of friends, i.e. corporate and creative. Although there are often exceptions, frequently the two just don't mix. Some of her closest friends simply "do not have a clue about what I do." Professionally, she has actually been asked why one would want so many of the "same thing." But she does not consider them to be "the same." Instead they are variations on a theme. The reasons so many people collect are fascinating and mysterious. Theories abound, with no two in agreement.

Collecting requires a great deal of time and work, and a large network of people who help and inspire you. It is extremely competitive today, as more and more people are getting in on the action. Often, much of the collecting is done very privately, as dealers save items for specific clients. The "under the table" policy can be helpful and frustrating at the same time, depending upon where you stand with a particular seller. The market and price situations fluctuate quickly and dramatically.

New collectors who stick with it are quickly indoctrinated into the game. An illustration of this might be the "lunch-box" collector looking for metal and vinyl lunch boxes from the '50s and '60s. At first, a collector can find lunch boxes easily, at relatively reasonable prices. As the collection begins to grow and the collector develops a deeper knowledge of the boxes, he begins to seek the rarer ones. Suddenly the collector realizes that these rarer boxes are much harder to find. He soon learns that the other lunch box collectors are looking for the same boxes; and although some are available from specialty dealers, there is now a whole new, and quite shocking, price range.

The collecting process must now be re-evaluated and a decision made on how to continue. You can either "pay the price" or hope that the item you seek shows up at a flea market for a bargain price. Or, and here is the secret, you can **trade**. Another collector may desperately need the box you found last week for $25, and in return will give you the one you saw at a show for $750. Needless to say, collectors are very big on trading.

Certain areas of collecting are "hot" for only a given time. This can be dictated by many variables from the fashion industry's latest focus, to the culture's latest fixation. Cowboy collectibles can be fueled by fashion. Hawaiiana can be influenced by a combination of fashion, the entertainment industry and collectors themselves.

Many variables affect a collectible's price. A new book on a specific area of collecting can readily cause a jolt in prices. It is all a part of the joys of collecting. Good luck with yours! It's fun.

BIBLIOGRAPHY

Bosker, Gideon, Michele Mancini, and John Gramstad. *Fabulous Fabrics of the 50s.* San Francisco: Chronicle Books, 1992.

Bougie, Stanley J. and David A. Newkirk. *Red Wing Dinnerware.*

Burns, Mark and Louis BuBonis. *Fifties Homestyle.* New York: Harper & Row Publishers, 1988.

Dorfles, Gillo. *Kitsch.* New York: Universe Books, 1969.

The Editors of Time-Life Books. *The Fabulous Century 1950-1960.* New York: Time-Life Books, 1970.

Greenberg, Cara. *Mid-Century Modern.* New York: Harmony Books, 1984.

Hillier, Bevis. *The Decorative Arts of the Forties and Fifties.* New York: Clarkson N. Potter, Inc., 1975.

Hillier, Bevis. *The Style of the Century 1900-1980.* London: The Herbert Press, 1983.

Hine, Thomas. *Populuxe.* New York: Alfred A. Knopf, 1986.

Horn, Richard. *Fifties Style Then and Now.* New York: Beech Tree Books, 1985.

Jackson, Lesley. *The New Look Design in the Fifties.* New York: Thames & Hudson, 1991.

Meller, Susan and Joost Elffers. *Textile Designs.* New York: Harry N. Abrams, Inc., 1991.

Sparke, Penny. *An Introduction to Design and Culture in the Twentieth Century.* New York: Harper & Row, 1986.

PRICE REFERENCE

Values vary immensely according to an article's condition, location of the market (flea markets or fancy shops), parts of the country, materials, craftmanship, rarity, demand and overall quality of the design. Market conditions of a specific category may be "hot," at the "peak" or "over." Sellers may be willing to negotiate, or not.

While collectors must make their own decisions, we can provide you with estimates from our survey of different markets, intended to act merely as a guide. Values are in U.S. dollars.

ACCESSORIES FOR THE HOME

Chapters 1-4

Art pottery of Sascha Brastoff $25-1000+

The items will vary in value according to differences in the designs, the rarity, the sizes and whether the piece is an original by the artist or just a product of his studio.

Drinking glasses, per set $20-150

Textiles, per yard $10-100+

Major factors affecting textile values include the designs, type of fabric, type of weave and the amount of yardage. Large amounts of yardage can either increase or decrease a price per yard; for example, a high price per yard may be asked if the yardage amount presents more choices of what can be done with the fabric, or a lower price per yard may be asked if the total price becomes too high. A seller may sometimes feel that if they do not get their price, they can use the fabric to recover furniture, and thereby increase the value of the furniture. Many dealers hoard textiles for this reason. Also, colors affect values; some are just more desirable. For example, black backgrounds will appeal to more people than brown backgrounds, as a general rule only.

There is no substitute for time and experience spent to gain judgement for determining the quality of textiles. You must handle them, train your eye and your fingers to slowly absorb what it is that makes the important differences. Continually feel the old fabrics and compare them with what is available today. No book or personal explanation can give you this knowledge. Your own experience is essential.

ART FROM THE CLOSET

Chapters 5-13

Lucite and vinyl handbags $25-500+

For lucite handbags, values are influenced by the sculptural quality of the piece as well as its rarity. Black handbags are desirable, and the addition of rhinestones is another bonus. Condition is a very important factor.

Vinyl handbags can be more valuable with different designs, especially if they are highly whimsical. Styles that are more typical of the period can influence a price, as can rarity.

Circle skirts $20-250+

The designs and fabrics of circle skirts affect their prices. If there is a great deal of added hand work, such as appliques, the price can be higher. Size can influence a circle skirt's price. Certain manufacturer's labels are sought after, but many skirts were home made.

Gabardine jackets and shirts $40-500+

The decorative designs on gabardine garments, such as the ever-popular diamond-motif, are important influences on pricing. Also, the number of colors used in the decoration affects the price; two, three or four-color articles are more desirable than solids. Besides that, specific colors and cmbinations are more popular: black and pink, and black and white especially. Red is particularly rare, while navy blue, beige and brown are more common colors. Nevertheless, a great design in navy blue might be more desirable than a poor design in black and white. Another consideration is the weight and quality of the gabardine; heavy gabardine drapes in a wonderful way that lighter weaves do not. The finest European gabardine made today does not compare with the high quality of the best gabardines made in the 1940s and '50s. The quality of the tailoring can also affect the price; try them on and you will see the difference. Not the least consideration is the size of a gabardine jacket or shirt. In the 1970s when men were collecting '50s garments, the style was for tight-fitting shirts and jackets, so size medium was most popular. Large, large, large is the cry today. Modern fashions call for loose-fitting, casual, comfortable clothing — and the larger the size, the more it fits this critieria for men and women alike.

Print rayon shirts (called "Hawaiian," "aloha," or "silkies" by many) $20-500+

Print rayon shirts are evaluated primarily by their designs and colors, with black backgrounds the most sought-after. The quality of the rayon is important too, and here there are endless varieties: heavy, drapy, silky (the author's personal favorite). Certain manufacturers are known for the highest quality, such as "Kamehameha." The condition of the fabric is also a factor; watch out for pin holes, and be sure to hold the garment up to the light. The number of repairs can affect the value. Shirts can be repaired without destroying the value if they are done right, but repairs should nonetheless be brought to the attention of buyers. Things to look for include small holes, resewn or replaced buttons and turned collars. If a shirt has never been worn or washed, it is in pristine condition and will be priced higher. You can expect certain dyes to have deteriorated over the years. And size again is an important factor in judging price; large size can double the value of high-end shirts. Certain prints are sought-after by all collectors, such as "Man Climbing Coconut Tree." Beware of shirts newly made from old fabric; these have flooded the market. Examine authentic, high quality shirts carefully to learn how they should look. Notice whether the inside seams are sewn double and the way the collars and pockets lay. Notice whether the buttons were sewn on by the factory; they look different from hand-sewn buttons. Note the width of the inside flaps. Borders should be the selvage of a fabric that will not unravel and does not need to be stitched. The reason for this is that early bolts of fabric were woven on narrower looms. When wider bolts were woven, the inside flap was often a cut piece which needed to be stitched down. Also, the later inside flaps are narrower. Better shirts have a seam across the back.

Hawaiian dresses $50-500

The particular print, size, color and condition all affect the value of a Hawaiian dress. Be aware that many dealers put high prices on dresses or don't even sell them. Instead they can always cut them up and make shirts from the cloth which generally sell for higher prices. Most serious collectors abhor this practice since the dresses should be preserved in their original state.

Rayon dresses $40-350

INSPIRED MOTIFS

Chapters 14-17

With all the special "inspired motifs," subject matter makes a difference. Certain subjects are just in great demand, like cowboy prints. The design quality always affects the price.

INDEX